ADHD KIDS 12 SUCCESS STORIES

STORIES OF KIDS WITH ADHD WHO
FOUND WHAT WORKS, INCLUDING
EASY ACTIVITIES AND STRATEGIES
FOR AGES 7-11

RICHARD BASS

Copyright Page

ADHD Kids: 12 Success Stories

Copyright © 2026 by Richard Bass

Published by RBG Publishing

First Edition: 2026

Disclaimer: This book is designed to provide information and motivation to readers. It is sold with the understanding that the author and publisher are not engaged to render any type of psychological, medical, legal, or any other kind of professional advice. The content is the sole expression and opinion of the author. No warranties or guarantees are expressed or implied by the choice to include any of the content in this book. Neither the publisher nor the author shall be liable for any physical, psychological, emotional, financial, or commercial damages, including but not limited to special, incidental, consequential, or other damages. You are responsible for your own choices, actions, and results.

The characters and stories in this book are fictional composites created for educational purposes. While they reflect common ADHD experiences and evidence-based strategies, they do not represent any specific individuals.

Medical Disclaimer

Important Notice to Readers

This book is intended for educational and informational purposes only. It is not intended to diagnose, treat, cure, or prevent any medical or psychological condition, including ADHD (Attention-Deficit/Hyperactivity Disorder).

Please note:

The stories in this book are fictional and designed to illustrate common ADHD challenges and evidence-based strategies for children. They are not substitutes for professional medical or mental health advice.

If you suspect your child has ADHD, please seek evaluation from a qualified healthcare provider, such as a pediatrician, child psychiatrist, psychologist, or licensed mental health professional.

The strategies discussed in this book are based on research and clinical best practices, but individual results may vary. What works for one child with ADHD may not work for another.

Medication decisions should always be made in consultation with a qualified healthcare provider who knows your child's individual medical history and needs.

If your child is experiencing a mental health crisis, please contact a mental health professional, call 988 (Suicide and Crisis Lifeline), or go to your nearest emergency room.

This book is meant to complement, not replace, the relationship you have with healthcare providers and mental health professionals.

Dedication

A Note to Parents

This book is written for kids ages 7-11 to read themselves or with you.

How to use this book with your child:

Reading together works best. While some older kids (ages 10-11) may read independently, most children in this age range benefit from reading with a parent. You can take turns reading aloud, discuss the stories as you go, and work through the activities together.

It's okay to read out of order. If your child is struggling most with sitting still, start with that story. If forgetting things is the biggest challenge, begin there. You don't have to read cover to cover.

The Think About It questions are for conversation. These aren't homework. They're starting points for you and your child to talk about their experiences. There are no wrong answers.

The Try This sections need your support. The strategies are designed to be simple, but elementary-age kids need parent involvement to implement them. You'll be an active partner in trying these strategies.

Keep it positive. ADHD is challenging, but this book emphasizes that kids with ADHD aren't broken, they're different. Help your child see their strengths alongside the challenges.

Be patient. Strategies take time to work. Your child won't master everything after one reading. This book is a resource you can return to as your child grows and faces new challenges.

Most importantly: Believe your child when they say something is hard. ADHD makes things genuinely more difficult, even when it doesn't look hard to you.

A Note to Kids

Hi! This book is for you.

If you have ADHD, you might feel like some things are really hard for you that seem easy for other kids.

Maybe you have trouble sitting still. Maybe you forget things a lot. Maybe you get in trouble for talking when you're not supposed to. Maybe big feelings sometimes feel TOO big.

Here's something important: You're not bad. You're not in trouble. Your brain just works differently.

In this book, you'll meet 12 kids who have ADHD just like you. They struggled with things, but they found ways to make things better. They learned that having ADHD doesn't mean you can't do great things. It just means you might need to do them differently.

After each story, there are questions called "Think About It" where you can think about your own experiences. Then there's a section called "Try This!" with one simple thing you can try to make things easier.

You can read this book by yourself if you're a good reader, or you can read it with a parent or teacher. Either way is great!

Remember: You're not alone. Lots of kids have ADHD. And you can learn to work with your brain instead of fighting against it.

Let's meet the first kid!

How to Use This Book

For Kids:

1. **Read the story.** You'll meet a kid with ADHD who has challenges you might recognize.
2. **Think about the questions.** After each story, there are 3 questions to help you think about your own experiences. You can think about them quietly, talk about them with a parent, or write down your answers if you want to.
3. **Try the activity!** Each story has one simple thing you can try this week. It's okay if it doesn't work perfectly the first time. That's normal!
4. **Pick what helps.** Not every strategy will work for you, and that's okay. Some will help a lot, some

might help a little, and some might not help at all. Keep the ones that work!

For Parents:

1. **Read together when possible.** Your involvement helps your child connect the stories to their own life.
2. **Use the questions as conversation starters.** The Think About It sections aren't tests. They're opportunities to understand your child's experience better.
3. **Implement strategies together.** The Try This sections require your active participation. You'll need to help set up systems, provide reminders, and support your child as they try new approaches.
4. **Be patient and celebrate small wins.** Change takes time. If your child successfully uses one strategy from one story, that's progress worth celebrating.
5. **Return to stories as needed.** If a new challenge emerges, revisit the relevant story. This book is a tool to use again and again.

Remember: ADHD looks different for every child. Your child might see themselves in every story or just a few. Both are normal!

Story 1: The Wiggle Problem

A story about learning that your body's need to move

isn't bad, and there are ways to wiggle that help instead of causing trouble.

Mia Chen's leg bounced under her desk. Bounce, bounce, bounce. She didn't mean to do it. Her leg just did it on its own.

"Mia, please sit still," Mrs. Taylor said.

Mia pressed her foot flat on the floor. She tried really hard. But one minute later, her leg was bouncing again.

The girl next to her whispered, "You're shaking the table."

"Sorry," Mia said. She tried to stop, but then her hands started tapping instead. Her body just didn't want to be still.

This happened every single day. At reading time, she wiggled. At lunch, she squirmed. During math, her pencil tapped and her feet swung.

"Mia, stop moving," her teacher would say. Over and over.

Mia would try. She would sit on her hands. She would cross her legs tight. But a few minutes later, she'd be moving again without even realizing it.

The other kids could sit still. They sat with their feet on the floor and their hands in their laps. Why couldn't Mia do that?

At home, dinner was hard too.

"Mia, please sit down," her mom said.

Mia sat, but two minutes later she was up getting a napkin. Then she was kneeling on her chair. Then she was swinging her legs so much her foot kicked the table.

"Mia!" her brother said. "You spilled my milk!"

"I didn't mean to!"

"You need to sit still like everyone else," her dad said.

Mia looked around the table. Everyone else WAS sitting still. Just her moving and wiggling.

That night, Mia cried in her room.

Why was sitting still so easy for everyone but so hard for her? She tried SO hard. Maybe something was wrong with her.

Her mom came in. "What's wrong, sweetie?"

"I can't sit still. I try and try, but I can't. I think I'm broken."

"Oh, Mia." Her mom gave her a hug. "You're not broken. Your brain works differently. You have ADHD. It means your body needs to move more than other kids. It's not bad. It's just different."

"But I get in trouble."

"I know. Let me talk to your teacher. We'll find ways for you to move that don't cause problems."

The next week, Mia's mom talked to Mrs. Taylor. When she came out, she was smiling.

"We have a plan! First, you're getting a special wiggle seat. It lets you move a little while you sit. Second, you can stand at the tall table in back if sitting feels too hard. And third, if you feel really wiggly, you can ask to do ten jumping jacks in the hallway."

"I can move and it's okay?" Mia asked.

"The right kind of moving, yes!"

The next day, Mia had a blue squishy cushion on her chair. When she sat on it, she could bounce a tiny bit. It felt good!

During math, she felt super wiggly. She raised her hand. "Can I stand at the back table?"

"Sure," Mrs. Taylor said.

Mia stood at the tall table doing her math. Her legs could move. She could shift and bounce on her toes. And her brain worked better when her body could move!

At home, her parents got her a wobble stool for homework. It rocked back and forth while she worked. At dinner, she could stand at the counter if sitting felt too hard, and she could take quick running breaks in the backyard.

"Your body needs to move," her mom said. "We're giving it good ways to move."

A few weeks later, Mia's friend Emma asked, "Why do you get that special cushion?"

"Because my body needs to move more than yours," Mia explained. "I have ADHD. Moving helps me focus."

"Can I try it?"

Emma sat on the wiggle cushion for a minute. "It IS bouncy! But I like regular chairs better."

"That's because your body is different from mine," Mia said. "My body needs to move. It's just how I am."

One day, a new kid joined the class. His name was Tyler. Mia noticed he wiggled a lot too.

At recess, she talked to him. "Do you have trouble sitting still?"

"Yeah. I get in trouble for it."

"Me too! I have ADHD. My body needs to move more. Do you have ADHD?"

"I don't know."

"You should tell your parents. I have special tools now that help. A wiggly cushion and I can stand at my desk. It makes school way easier."

"Really?"

"Really. Moving isn't bad. Some bodies just need it more."

At the end of the year, Mrs. Taylor asked Mia to stay after class.

"Mia, you've done great this year. I also want to say I'm sorry I kept telling you to sit still at the beginning. I didn't understand your body needs to move. I learned from you this year."

"You did?"

"I did. I learned kids are all different. Some need to move to focus. Thank you for teaching me."

Mia smiled big. She had taught her teacher something!

That summer at the park, Mia ran and climbed and played for hours. Her brother sat on a bench reading.

"Don't you want to run?" she asked.

"Nah, I'm good here."

Her brother liked sitting and reading. She liked moving and playing. They were just different.

And different was okay.

Mia climbed to the top of the jungle gym and thought about how much had changed. She still wiggled. She still needed to move. But now she had tools that helped. Now people understood.

Her wiggly body wasn't bad. It was just different. And with the right tools, she could be wiggly AND do well in school.

She could be herself.

THINK ABOUT IT

1. **Mia's body always wanted to move, even when she tried really hard to sit still. Does your body feel like this too?** What happens when you try to sit still for a long time?

2. **Mia felt bad because she thought something was wrong with her. Have you ever felt that way because something easy for other kids is hard for you?**

3. **Mia learned that moving isn't bad, her body just needs it more. What helps YOUR body feel better?** (Moving? Squeezing something? Taking breaks?)

TRY THIS!

This week, try adding movement to help your body and brain.

Your ADHD body might need to move to help your brain focus. That's okay! The trick is finding ways to move that don't get you in trouble.

At school (ask your teacher or parent to help):

- Ask for something to squeeze during class (a squishy ball or smooth stone)
- See if you can stand while you work sometimes
- When you feel really wiggly, ask for a quick movement break (10 jumping jacks or walk to get water)

At home during homework:

- Sit on a yoga ball or cushion that lets you move

- Stand at a counter instead of sitting
- Take a 5-minute movement break after every 15 minutes of work (run outside, jump, dance)

Try this for one week. Notice if moving helps you focus better!

Remember: Your wiggly body isn't bad. You're not in trouble. Your body just works differently, and that's okay!

Story 2: The Forget-It Kid

A story about learning that when your brain doesn't remember well, you can use tools to remember for you.

Jamal Williams forgot his homework again.

He KNEW he had homework. He remembered doing it last night at the kitchen table. But this morning, when he packed his backpack, he couldn't find it anywhere.

"Jamal, time for school!" his mom called.

"I can't find my homework!"

His mom sighed. "Did you check your folder?"

Jamal looked in his folder. Not there. He looked in his desk. Not there. He looked under his bed. There it was! But now they were late.

At school, his teacher Mrs. Lopez frowned. "Jamal, where's your math homework?"

"I forgot it at home. I did it, I promise!"

"That's the third time this week."

Jamal felt his face get hot. He HAD done the homework. Why did he keep forgetting to bring it?

Forgetting was Jamal's biggest problem.

He forgot his lunch box at school. He forgot his jacket at recess. He forgot what his teacher just said two minutes ago.

His mom would say, "Jamal, go upstairs and get your shoes." By the time he got upstairs, he'd forgotten why he went there. He'd stand in his room thinking, "Why did I come up here?"

"ADHD makes your brain forget things faster," his mom explained. "It's called working memory. Your brain doesn't hold onto information as well as other kids."

"But I TRY to remember!"

"I know you do, honey. But trying harder doesn't fix working memory. We need to use tools instead."

That weekend, Jamal's dad sat with him. His dad had ADHD too.

"When I was your age, I forgot stuff all the time," his dad said. "I still do! But I learned to use brain helpers."

"What's a brain helper?"

"Tools that remember FOR you, so your brain doesn't have to. Watch."

His dad pulled out his phone. "I don't try to remember my grocery list. I write it in my phone. See? Milk, bread, eggs. My phone remembers so I don't have to."

"But I don't have a phone."

"You have other tools. Let me show you."

They got a special folder for Jamal's homework. It was bright red so it was easy to see.

"ALL homework goes in this folder as soon as you finish it," his dad said. "Not later. Right when you're done. Then the folder stays in your backpack. Always."

"What if I forget to put it in the folder?"

"We'll put a big sign on the table that says PUT HOME-WORK IN RED FOLDER. The sign remembers for you."

His dad helped him make more brain helpers.

By the door, they put a basket. "Every day when you come home, your backpack goes in this basket. Not on the floor, not in your room. In the basket. That way you always know where it is."

They made a checklist with pictures. It showed: homework folder, lunch box, jacket, shoes. "Before you leave for school, check the list. The list remembers for you."

At school, Mrs. Lopez let Jamal take pictures of the homework board with a tablet. "Instead of trying to remember what I wrote, take a picture. Then you have it."

Jamal felt weird using all these tools. Other kids didn't need them.

"Other kids have better working memory," his dad said. "You have different tools. That's okay. Everybody's brain is different."

The first week was hard. Jamal kept forgetting to use his brain helpers!

On Monday, he did his homework but forgot to put it in the red folder. His mom found it on his desk. "Remember, homework goes right in the folder."

On Tuesday, he put his homework in the folder! But then he left his backpack in the car.

On Wednesday, he remembered everything! His homework was in the folder, his backpack was ready, he checked his picture of the homework board.

"You did it!" his mom said.

By Friday, Jamal was getting better at using his tools. The more he used them, the easier they got.

At school, some kids noticed Jamal's red folder.

"Why is your folder red?" asked his friend Miguel.

"So I can find it easy. I have ADHD and I forget stuff a lot. The bright color helps me remember."

"Oh. That's smart."

When Mrs. Lopez wrote homework on the board, Jamal raised his hand. "Can I take a picture?"

"Sure, Jamal."

He took a picture with the class tablet. Now he didn't have to remember the assignment. The picture remembered for him.

That night, he checked his picture and did all his homework. He put it right in the red folder. The next morning, he checked his checklist by the door: homework folder, lunch box, jacket.

He had everything!

At school, he turned in his homework with everyone else.

Mrs. Lopez smiled. "Great job, Jamal!"

Jamal still forgot things sometimes. One day he forgot his library book. Another day he forgot it was pizza day and brought a regular lunch.

But he was forgetting WAY less than before.

"How come you're not forgetting stuff as much?" Miguel asked.

"I use brain helpers. Like this checklist by my door. And I take pictures of homework instead of trying to remember it. And all my homework goes in one red folder so I can't lose it."

"Does it work?"

"Yeah! I still forget sometimes. But not as much."

One day, Jamal's mom said, "Go get your library book from your room."

Jamal went upstairs. But when he got to his room, he stopped. "Why did I come up here?"

He'd forgotten again!

Instead of feeling bad, Jamal went back downstairs. "Mom, I forgot. Can you tell me again?"

"Library book from your room."

This time, Jamal repeated it out loud as he walked. "Library book, library book, library book." He found it!

His dad high-fived him. "See? When you forget, you ask again. That's using your brain helpers too."

At the end of the year, Jamal looked at his red homework folder. It was worn and a little torn, but it had worked! He'd turned in his homework almost every day.

He thought about the beginning of the year when he forgot things constantly and got in trouble all the time.

Now he had tools. A red folder. A checklist. Pictures of the homework board. A basket for his backpack.

He still forgot things. His working memory was still not as good as other kids. But now he didn't TRY to remember every-thing. He let his tools remember for him.

That summer, Jamal's family went on vacation. In the car, his mom said, "Jamal, don't forget your tablet."

"I won't!" He grabbed his tablet and put it in his special travel bag right away.

His little sister said, "How come you never forget stuff anymore?"

"Oh, I still forget. But I use brain helpers. Tools that remember for me. See this bag? I put everything I need in it right away, so I don't have to remember later."

"That's smart."

"My brain doesn't remember good. But my tools remember great!"

And that was okay.

THINK ABOUT IT

1. **Jamal forgot things all the time, even when he tried really hard to remember. Do you forget things a lot too?** What kinds of things do you forget most?

2. **Jamal felt bad when people thought he wasn't trying, but he WAS trying. Have you felt that way when people don't believe you?**

3. **Jamal learned to use "brain helpers" like folders and checklists that remember FOR him. What tools might help YOU remember things?**

TRY THIS!

This week, try using one "brain helper" to remember for you.

Your ADHD brain might not hold onto information well. That's okay! Instead of trying harder to remember, you can use tools that remember FOR you.

Pick ONE of these brain helpers to try:
For homework:

- Get one special folder (bright color!) where ALL homework goes as soon as you finish it
- Keep the folder in your backpack always
- Ask a parent to help remind you: "Is your homework in the folder?"

For morning routine:

- Make a checklist with pictures of what you need (homework, lunch, jacket, etc.)
- Put it by the door
- Check it every morning before school

For things you need to remember:

- Ask a parent to help you take a picture of important stuff (like the homework board)
- Pictures help you remember without using your brain!

Try ONE of these for a whole week. It might feel weird at first. That's normal! The more you use it, the easier it gets.

Remember: Your brain doesn't remember well. That's not your fault! Using tools isn't cheating. It's smart!

Story 3: The Distraction Queen

A story about learning that when everything distracts you, you can change your space to help you focus.

Lily Martinez was supposed to be doing her math worksheet. But a bird just landed outside the window. A blue bird! Was it a blue jay?

"Lily, eyes on your paper," Mrs. Chen said.

Lily looked back at her worksheet. 5 + 3 = ... what was she doing again? Oh right, math.

5 + 3 = 8. She wrote it down.

Then she heard someone laugh in the hallway. Who was that? What was funny?

She looked at the clock. How much time until recess?

She noticed her friend Emma had a sparkly eraser. So shiny!

"Lily!" Mrs. Chen said. "Focus, please."

Lily jumped. She looked at her paper. She'd only done two problems and math time was almost over. Where did the time go?

This happened every single day. Lily would start her work, but then something would catch her attention. A noise. A movement. A thought in her own head. Before she knew it, everyone else was done and Lily had barely started.

At home, it was the same.

"Time for homework," her mom said.

Lily sat at the kitchen table with her reading book. She started reading. But then she heard the TV in the other room. What show was that?

She saw her cat walk by. "Fluffy!" She petted him for a minute.

She noticed a drawing she'd made yesterday. She picked it up to look at it.

"Lily, you've been sitting there for twenty minutes and you're still on the first page," her mom said.

"I'm trying!"

"You need to focus."

But Lily didn't know HOW to focus. Everything around her was so interesting! How did other kids ignore all the interesting stuff?

That weekend, Lily's mom talked to her about ADHD.

"Your brain notices EVERYTHING," her mom explained. "Most kids' brains filter out stuff that's not important. But your ADHD brain notices the bird, and the sound, and the shiny eraser, and everything. It's all interesting to your brain."

"Is that bad?"

"It's not bad. But it makes it hard to focus on boring stuff like math worksheets. We need to make your space less distracting."

"How?"

"By taking away things that catch your attention. Watch."

They went to Lily's room. Her mom helped her move her desk away from the window. "Now you won't see birds and cars and people walking by."

They put her toys in the closet and closed the door. "Now you won't see them when you're trying to do homework."

They got her special headphones. "You can play quiet music. It blocks out other sounds that distract you."

"But what if I get distracted by my own thoughts?"

"We'll work on that too. Let's try a timer. You work for ten minutes, then you get a break. Ten minutes isn't very long. Your brain can focus for ten minutes."

On Monday, Lily tried her new setup at home.

Her desk faced the wall, not the window. Her toys were hidden. She put on her headphones with soft music.

Her mom set a timer for ten minutes. "Read until the timer beeps. That's all."

Lily opened her book. She started reading. She heard a noise, but the music in her headphones blocked it out. She thought about her cat, but then she remembered: just ten minutes. She could do ten minutes.

The timer beeped! She'd read for ten whole minutes without getting distracted!

"Good job!" her mom said. "Take a five minute break, then we'll do another ten minutes."

At school, Mrs. Chen let Lily move to a desk at the back of the room where there was less to see. She gave Lily a special folder to put over her worksheet so she could only see the problem she was working on, not all the other problems that made her brain jump around.

She also let Lily use soft earplugs during quiet work time. They didn't block out her teacher's voice, but they did block out pencils tapping and people whispering and all the little noises that pulled Lily's attention away.

The first week was better! Lily got more work done than usual.

But on Friday, she got distracted by her own thoughts. She was doing math, but then she started thinking about her birthday party next month. What kind of cake would she get? Who would she invite? What games would they play?

When the timer beeped, she'd only done three math problems.

"My thoughts distracted me," she told her mom.

"That's called daydreaming. A lot of ADHD brains do that. Let's try something. When you notice your brain wandering to other thoughts, just say 'not now' and look back at your work.

You're not in trouble for daydreaming. Just notice it and come back."

Lily tried it. On Monday, during reading, her brain started thinking about the movie she watched yesterday. She noticed and thought, "Not now, brain." She went back to reading.

It worked!

After a few weeks, Lily had a routine. At home, she worked at her desk facing the wall with her headphones on. She used a timer for ten-minute chunks. When her brain wandered to other thoughts, she said "not now" and came back.

At school, she sat in the back where there was less to see. She used her folder to cover extra problems. She wore soft earplugs during quiet work.

She still got distracted sometimes. But way less than before.

One day, Emma asked, "Why do you sit in the back now?"

"Because I have ADHD and I notice everything. Sitting back here means there's less stuff to distract me. It helps me focus."

"Oh. Does it work?"

"Yeah! I get my work done faster now."

At the end of the year, Lily's report card said she'd improved so much in finishing her work on time.

That night, her mom gave her a high five. "You did it! You learned to manage distractions."

"I still get distracted."

"I know. But now you have tools. You know how to set up your space to help your brain focus. That's a big deal!"

Lily thought about it. At the beginning of the year, she'd been distracted by everything all the time. She barely finished any work.

Now she had a special spot with less distractions. She had headphones to block noise. She had a timer to help her focus for short chunks. She had a folder to cover extra stuff on her paper. And she knew how to notice when her brain wandered and bring it back.

She still noticed more than other kids. At recess, she noticed cool clouds and interesting bugs and birds singing. Her friends didn't notice that stuff.

"Your brain notices a lot," her mom said. "That's not bad. When you're playing or exploring, noticing everything is great! You just needed to learn how to focus when you needed to."

And now she could.

THINK ABOUT IT

1. **Lily got distracted by everything around her and by her own thoughts. Does this happen to you too? What distracts you most?**
2. **Lily felt frustrated because other kids could focus easily. Have you felt that way when something is hard for you but easy for others?**

3. **Lily learned that changing her space (moving her desk, using headphones, covering extra stuff) helped her focus. What might help YOU have fewer distractions?**

TRY THIS!

This week, try making your homework space less distracting.

Your ADHD brain notices EVERYTHING. That's not bad! But it makes focusing hard. You can make it easier by changing your space.

Try these at home (ask a parent to help):

Make your space boring:

- Do homework away from windows, toys, and TV
- Face a blank wall if possible
- Put away anything shiny, colorful, or interesting while you work

Block out sounds:

- Use headphones with quiet music or white noise
- Or use soft earplugs (you can still hear, but less)

Use a timer:

- Work for 10 minutes, then take a 3-minute break

- It's easier to focus when you know a break is coming!

Cover extra stuff:

- Use a paper to cover problems you're not working on yet
- Your brain won't jump ahead to other problems

Try these tools for one week. See if having fewer distractions helps you get your work done faster!

Remember: Your brain notices everything. That's okay! You just need the right space to help you focus when you need to.

STORY 4: THE BLURT-OUT BOY

A story about learning that you can pause for three seconds before speaking, and your thought won't

disappear.

Carlos Rodriguez's hand shot up in class.

"Yes, Carlos?" Mrs. Davis said.

"The answer is twelve!" Carlos said.

Mrs. Davis sighed. "Carlos, I hadn't finished asking the question yet."

"Oh. Sorry."

Carlos felt his face get hot. He did it again. The answer had felt so urgent in his brain that it just came flying out of his mouth before he could stop it.

At lunch, his friend Sophia was telling a story. "And then my cat climbed up the..."

"I have a cat too!" Carlos interrupted. "His name is Whiskers and he's orange and..."

Sophia frowned. "I wasn't done talking."

"Sorry! I just remembered about my cat."

Later at recess, kids were picking teams for kickball. Carlos shouted, "I want to be captain!"

"Carlos, we were doing rock-paper-scissors to pick," a kid said. "You can't just yell."

Carlos felt frustrated. Why did he keep talking at the wrong time? He didn't mean to be rude!

At home, it was the same.

His family was eating dinner. His sister was talking. "Today in science, we learned about..."

"I learned about planets!" Carlos blurted. "Did you know Jupiter is the biggest..."

"Carlos!" his dad said. "Your sister was talking. You need to wait your turn."

"But I had something to say!"

"You always have something to say," his sister muttered. "You never let anyone finish."

Carlos felt bad. He didn't want to be rude. But the thoughts in his head felt so important. If he didn't say them RIGHT NOW, they might disappear!

That night, Carlos's mom came to his room. "I know you don't mean to interrupt. Your ADHD brain makes thoughts feel urgent. Like if you don't say them immediately, they'll vanish."

"They WILL vanish!" Carlos said.

"Actually, they won't. That's your ADHD brain lying to you. Thoughts don't disappear in three seconds. But I know it FEELS like they will. We need to teach your brain to wait."

The next day, Carlos's mom taught him a trick.

"When you have something to say, before you say it, squeeze your hands together and count to three. One, two, three. Then you can talk."

"But what if I forget what I was going to say?"

"If you forget in three seconds, it probably wasn't that important. But you probably won't forget. Try it."

They practiced. Carlos had a thought. He squeezed his hands. One, two, three. Then he spoke.

"See? The thought didn't disappear!"

At school, Mrs. Davis gave Carlos a special signal. If she saw his hand up and he looked like he might blurt, she'd hold up three fingers. That meant: wait three seconds.

Carlos saw her signal. He squeezed his hands. One, two, three. Then Mrs. Davis called on him.

"Good job waiting, Carlos!"

It was hard. Those three seconds felt SO long. His brain was screaming, "Say it NOW! Say it NOW!"

But he waited. And the thought didn't disappear.

At dinner that night, Carlos's sister was talking. Carlos opened his mouth to interrupt, but then he remembered. Squeeze and count. One, two, three.

His sister finished her sentence. Then Carlos raised his hand like they were in class.

His family laughed, but his dad said, "You can talk now, Carlos."

"I was going to say something about planets, but I waited!"

"I'm proud of you for waiting. What about planets?"

Carlos told them his fact. And it felt better because people were actually listening, not annoyed at him for interrupting.

Waiting was hard. Sometimes Carlos forgot and blurted anyway. But he was getting better.

At school, a girl named Keisha was reading her story out loud. Carlos thought of something funny to say. His mouth opened.

Wait. Squeeze and count. One, two, three.

Keisha finished reading. Then Carlos raised his hand. "I have a question!"

"Yes, Carlos?"

He asked his question. Mrs. Davis smiled. "Great question, and thank you for waiting until Keisha was done."

At recess, kids were talking about a movie. Carlos hadn't seen it, but he wanted to talk about a DIFFERENT movie. He opened his mouth.

Wait. Three seconds.

He let them finish talking about their movie. Then he said, "I saw a different movie. Want to hear about it?"

"Sure!" they said.

It felt good when people actually listened because he wasn't interrupting them.

After a few weeks, Carlos was waiting more and blurting less. It still felt hard. Waiting three seconds felt like forever to his ADHD brain.

But he noticed something. When he waited, people listened better. When he blurted, people got annoyed.

One day, his teacher was talking about homework. Carlos's hand went up. He had a question! It felt urgent!

But he saw Mrs. Davis's three-finger signal. He squeezed his hands. One, two, three.

Mrs. Davis finished explaining. Then she called on him. "Yes, Carlos?"

He asked his question.

"Great question! I'm glad you waited to ask."

That afternoon, Sophia told him, "You're getting better at not interrupting."

"Really?"

"Yeah. At the beginning of the year, you interrupted all the time. Now you wait. It's nice."

Carlos felt proud. His brain still made thoughts feel super

urgent. But he was learning that three seconds wouldn't make them disappear.

At the end of the year, Carlos's report card said, "Carlos has improved greatly in waiting his turn to speak."

His mom hugged him. "You worked so hard on this!"

"It's still hard," Carlos admitted. "My brain still wants to talk RIGHT NOW."

"I know. But you learned to wait anyway. That takes real effort with an ADHD brain."

That summer, Carlos and his family went to visit his grandparents. At dinner, everyone was talking. Carlos had SO many things to say!

But he remembered. Squeeze and count. Wait his turn. Let people finish.

When it was his turn to talk, everyone listened. His grandpa said, "Carlos, you've become such a good listener! You let everyone finish before you talk now."

Carlos smiled. He wasn't perfect. He still blurted sometimes. But he was getting better.

His thoughts didn't disappear in three seconds. They never had. His ADHD brain had been lying to him.

And now he knew the truth.

THINK ABOUT IT

1. **Carlos blurted out answers and interrupted people because his thoughts felt SO urgent. Do your thoughts feel like that too?** Like you HAVE to say them right away?
2. **Carlos worried that if he waited, he'd forget what he wanted to say. Have you felt that way?**
3. **Carlos learned to squeeze his hands and count to three before talking. Do you think this might help you, or would something else work better?**

TRY THIS!

This week, try the "squeeze and count to three" trick before you speak.

Your ADHD brain makes thoughts feel urgent, like they'll disappear if you don't say them RIGHT NOW. But that's not true! Your thoughts don't disappear in three seconds.

Here's what to do:

When you have something to say:

- Squeeze your hands together
- Count in your head: one, two, three
- THEN talk

This helps you:

- Pause before interrupting

- Wait for your turn
- Make sure it's a good time to talk

Practice at home first:

- At dinner, squeeze and count before talking
- When someone is telling a story, wait for them to finish
- Ask a parent to remind you if you forget

Then try at school:

- Count to three before raising your hand
- Wait for the teacher to call on you
- Let other kids finish talking first

Try this for one week. It will feel hard at first! Your brain will say "TALK NOW!" But wait anyway. You'll see that your thoughts don't disappear.

Remember: Waiting three seconds doesn't make you forget. It helps people listen better when you DO talk!

Story 5: The Too-Big Feelings

A story about learning that when feelings get huge, you can catch them early and calm down before they explode.

Emma Thompson lost the board game. Again.

"I HATE this game!" she yelled. She threw the dice across the room and ran to her room crying.

Her brother Jake shook his head. "It's just a game."

But to Emma, it wasn't just a game. Losing felt TERRI-BLE. Like the worst thing ever.

In her room, Emma cried hard. Her mom came in and hugged her.

"It was just a game, sweetie."

"I know," Emma sobbed. "But it felt so bad!"

This happened a lot. Emma's feelings were BIG. When she was happy, she was SUPER happy. When she was sad, she was SUPER sad. When she was angry, she was SUPER angry.

Yesterday, she'd gotten frustrated with her homework and ripped up her paper. This morning, she'd cried because her favorite shirt was dirty. At school last week, she'd yelled at her friend over something small and felt terrible after.

"Why do my feelings get so big?" Emma asked her mom.

"ADHD can make feelings extra strong. It's like the volume is turned way up. You feel things more than other kids do."

"But I don't want to!"

"I know. But we can learn to notice when feelings are getting big BEFORE they explode."

The next week, Emma's mom took her to see Mrs. Rivera, a counselor who helped kids with ADHD.

Mrs. Rivera showed Emma a picture of a thermometer, but

instead of temperature, it showed feelings numbers from 1 to 10.

"1 is calm. 5 is starting to feel big. 10 is explosion. When you threw the dice, you were at 10, right?"

Emma nodded.

"The trick is to notice when you're at 5 or 6. That's BEFORE the explosion. At 5, you can still calm down. At 10, it's much harder."

"How do I notice?"

"Your body gives you clues. Let's figure out YOUR clues."

They talked about what Emma felt before she exploded. Her chest felt tight. Her face felt hot. Her hands made fists. Her breath got faster.

"Those are your warning signs! When you notice those, you're probably at 5 or 6. That's when you use your calming tools."

"What calming tools?"

Mrs. Rivera taught her some:

- Take five deep breaths, slow and calm
- Get a drink of cold water
- Hug a stuffed animal tight
- Ask for a hug from a grown-up
- Take a break and go to a quiet space

"When you notice you're at 5, use one of these tools. Don't wait until you're at 10."

That week, Emma practiced.

At school, another kid accidentally bumped her in line. Emma felt angry. Her face felt hot. Her fists clenched.

Wait. Those were her warning signs! She was at 5!

Emma took five deep breaths. Slow. In and out.

The angry feeling got smaller. She was okay.

At home, she was doing homework and it was hard. She felt frustrated. Her chest felt tight.

Warning sign! She was at 5!

"Mom, I need a break," Emma said.

"Good job noticing! Go get a drink of water and hug your stuffed bear. Then we'll try again."

Emma did. When she came back, the frustration was smaller. She could keep working.

It didn't always work. Sometimes Emma didn't notice until she was already at 9 or 10, and then the feelings exploded anyway.

One day at recess, a girl said Emma's drawing was bad. Emma's face got hot, her chest got tight, and before she could stop it, she yelled, "YOUR drawings are worse!"

She ran to the bathroom and cried.

The counselor found her. "What happened?"

"I got to 10 before I noticed."

"That happens sometimes. The more you practice, the better you'll get at noticing at 5. But even when you get to 10, you can still calm down after. You did the right thing by coming here to calm down instead of yelling more."

Emma felt a little better.

After a few weeks, Emma was catching her feelings earlier more often.

Playing a board game with Jake, she started losing. She felt frustrated. Her chest got tight.

Warning! She was at 5!

"I need a break for a minute," she said. She went to her room, hugged her bear, and took deep breaths.

When she came back, she could play without exploding.

"You didn't throw the dice this time!" Jake said, surprised.

"I caught my feelings before they got too big."

At school, her friend forgot to save her a seat at lunch. Emma felt sad and a little angry. Her face felt hot.

Warning!

Emma took deep breaths. She got a drink of water. Then she calmly said, "Can you save me a seat next time?"

"Oh! Sorry, I forgot. I'll remember tomorrow."

Emma felt proud. She'd felt sad, but she hadn't exploded.

Mrs. Rivera told her parents, "Emma is doing great. She's learning to recognize her feelings at 5 instead of waiting until 10. That's a hard skill for ADHD brains."

"Are her feelings going to get less big?" her dad asked.

"No. She'll always feel things strongly. That's part of how her brain works. But she's learning to manage the big feelings before they explode. That's what matters."

Emma felt better knowing her big feelings weren't bad. They were just part of her. And she was learning to work with them.

At the end of third grade, Emma's teacher said, "Emma, you've done such a good job this year managing your emotions. I'm proud of you."

Emma smiled. At the beginning of the year, she'd cried or yelled almost every day. Now she could usually catch her feelings at 5 and calm down before they exploded.

She still had big feelings. That didn't change. When she was happy, she was SUPER happy. When she was sad, she was SUPER sad.

But now she had tools. She could notice the warning signs. She could use deep breaths, cold water, hugs, and breaks. She could calm down before the explosion.

That summer, Emma's family went to an amusement park. Emma got scared on a big roller coaster. Her chest felt tight. Her breath got fast.

Warning! She was at 6!

"Dad, I'm scared!" she said.

"Do you want to get off?"

"No, I want to ride it. But can you hold my hand? And can I take some deep breaths first?"

Her dad held her hand. Emma took five slow, deep breaths.

She still felt scared (maybe a 4 now instead of 6). But she could handle a 4. She rode the roller coaster and it was fun!

On the car ride home, her mom said, "You managed your big feelings so well today."

"I still have big feelings," Emma said. "But now I can handle them."

And that made all the difference.

THINK ABOUT IT

1. **Emma's feelings got SO big that she cried or yelled over things that didn't seem that big to**

other people. Do your feelings get really big like that?

2. **Emma's body gave her warning signs when feelings were getting big (hot face, tight chest, clenched fists). What does YOUR body feel like when your feelings are getting too big?**

3. **Emma learned tools to calm down like deep breaths, cold water, and hugs. What helps YOU calm down when you're upset?**

TRY THIS!

This week, learn to notice when your feelings are getting big BEFORE they explode.

Your ADHD brain makes feelings extra strong. That's okay! But you can learn to catch big feelings early and calm down before they get too huge.

Make your own feelings thermometer:

- 1-2 = Calm, feeling okay
- 3-4 = Starting to feel something (a little sad, frustrated, or angry)
- 5-6 = Feelings getting bigger (THIS is when to use your tools!)
- 7-8 = Feelings very big, hard to think clearly
- 9-10 = EXPLOSION (crying, yelling, throwing things)

Find YOUR warning signs (ask a parent to help):

- What does your body feel like at 5-6?
- Hot face? Tight chest? Fast breathing? Clenched fists?
- These are your early warning signs!

Pick 2-3 calming tools:

- Five slow deep breaths
- Drink of cold water
- Tight hug (stuffed animal or person)
- Take a break in a quiet spot
- Squeeze something soft

This week, practice:

- When you notice your warning signs, stop and check: "Am I at 5?"
- If yes, use one of your calming tools RIGHT THEN
- Don't wait until you're at 9 or 10!

Remember: Big feelings aren't bad. You're not in trouble for feeling them. You're just learning to catch them early so they don't explode!

Story 6: The Daydream Drifter

A story about learning that when your mind wanders, you can notice and bring it back.

Noah Park was listening to his teacher explain fractions. Or at least, he was TRYING to listen.

Mrs. Lee was talking about dividing pizzas into pieces. Noah was looking right at her. But his brain started thinking about pizza. Real pizza. The pizza place near his house had really good pepperoni pizza. Maybe his family could get pizza this weekend. What toppings would they get? Maybe pepperoni and mushrooms...

"Noah? Noah!"

Noah jumped. Mrs. Lee was looking at him. So was everyone else.

"Can you tell us what I just said?"

Noah's mind went blank. He'd been listening! Or... wait. Had he? He remembered pizza. But fractions?

"Um... pizza?" Noah said quietly.

Some kids giggled. Noah felt his face get hot.

"I was explaining how to find equivalent fractions," Mrs. Lee said gently. "Were you paying attention?"

"I was trying to."

But the truth was, his brain had drifted away and he hadn't even noticed until Mrs. Lee called his name.

This happened to Noah all the time. His brain would wander off without asking permission.

He'd be reading a book about dolphins, and suddenly he'd be thinking about the swimming pool, and then about his swimming lessons, and then about what he had for breakfast, and then he'd realize he'd read two whole pages without knowing what they said.

He'd be eating dinner, and someone would be talking, and Noah would look like he was listening, but really his brain was thinking about his Lego set upstairs, and when they asked him a question, he'd have no idea what they were talking about.

His teacher thought he wasn't paying attention on purpose. His parents thought he wasn't listening. But Noah WAS trying! His brain just kept... leaving.

That weekend, Noah's dad sat with him.

"I do the same thing," his dad said. "When I was your age, my brain wandered all the time. It still does! It's part of ADHD."

"Really?"

"Yep. ADHD brains are like puppies. They wander off to sniff interesting things without even telling you. You're listening to your teacher, but then your brain sees something interesting and chases it."

"Can I make it stop?"

"Not completely. But you can learn to notice when it happens and bring it back. Like calling a puppy back when it wanders."

Noah's dad taught him some tricks.

"When you're listening to someone talk, do something with

your hands. Doodle, or squeeze a stress ball, or take notes. It sounds weird, but keeping your hands busy helps your brain stay focused."

"Won't doodling distract me MORE?"

"Nope! For ADHD brains, doodling actually helps. Try it."

At school, Mrs. Lee let Noah doodle on a special paper while she taught. At first, it felt weird. But Noah noticed his brain wandered less! The doodling kept part of his brain busy so the listening part could focus.

Noah's dad also taught him to check in with himself. "Every few minutes, ask yourself: Am I still here? Am I listening? If your brain wandered, just bring it back. You're not in trouble. Just notice and come back."

During reading time, Noah tried it. He read a few sentences, then stopped. "Am I still here? Am I paying attention to the words?"

Yes, he was!

He read a few more sentences. Then checked again. "Am I still here?"

This time, he realized he'd been thinking about his video game instead of reading. He hadn't even noticed until he checked!

"Okay, brain. Come back." He reread the last few sentences and kept going.

It was like his dad said. His brain was like a puppy that kept wandering. But now Noah was learning to notice and call it back.

Mrs. Lee also helped. She started checking in with Noah more often during lessons. "Noah, can you repeat what I just said?"

It wasn't to get him in trouble. It was to help him notice when his brain wandered.

Sometimes Noah could repeat it. Sometimes he'd realize he'd drifted. "I'm sorry, I missed that part."

"That's okay. I'll say it again. Try to stay with me."

Noah tried. When Mrs. Lee was teaching, he doodled on his paper and checked in with himself every minute or so. "Am I still listening? Or did my brain wander?"

He caught himself wandering a lot at first. But catching it was the point! Each time he noticed and came back, he was practicing.

At home during homework, Noah's mom helped him practice too.

"Read this page, but stop halfway through and ask yourself if you know what you just read. If you don't, that means your brain wandered."

Noah tried it. He read half a page, then stopped. "Did I understand that?"

He had! He kept reading.

When he got to the end of the page, he checked again. This

time, he realized he'd been thinking about lunch instead of reading the last paragraph.

"My brain wandered."

"That's okay! You noticed. Now read it again."

Noticing was the first step. The more he practiced noticing, the better he got at catching his brain before it drifted too far away.

After a few weeks, Noah was getting better at staying focused. He still drifted sometimes. But now he noticed faster and brought his attention back.

One day in class, Mrs. Lee was explaining science. Noah was listening and doodling. Halfway through, he checked in with himself. "Am I still here?"

He realized he'd started thinking about recess. His brain had wandered!

He took a breath and looked back at Mrs. Lee. He focused on her words. His brain came back.

At the end of class, Mrs. Lee said, "Today we learned about the water cycle. Who can tell me the three parts?"

Noah raised his hand. He actually KNEW! Because he'd caught his brain wandering and brought it back before he missed too much.

At home, Noah's dad asked, "How's school?"

"Better! I'm getting better at noticing when my brain wanders."

"That's great! You know, your brain wandering isn't always bad. When you're playing or being creative, letting your brain wander is good. It's only a problem when you NEED to focus."

Noah thought about that. At recess, he'd be playing and his brain would jump from idea to idea. That was fun! When he was building with Legos, his brain would imagine cool things. That was creative!

The wandering brain was only a problem during class or homework, when he needed to focus on specific things.

"So I don't need to stop my brain from wandering ALL the time?"

"Nope. Just when it matters. And you're learning when it matters and how to bring it back. That's the important part."

At the end of the year, Noah's report card said he'd improved in paying attention during lessons.

That night, his mom hugged him. "You worked hard on this!"

"I still daydream sometimes."

"Everyone daydreams! But you're better at noticing and coming back. That's what counts."

That summer, Noah went to the library and checked out books about space. He loved space! He could read about planets and stars for hours.

Sometimes while reading, his brain would wander to other things. But now he'd notice. "Oops, came back, brain." And he'd keep reading.

His brain was still like a puppy that wandered off. But now Noah knew how to call it back.

And that made all the difference.

THINK ABOUT IT

1. **Noah's mind would wander away without him noticing until someone called his name. Does your mind wander like that?** What do you think about when your mind drifts?

2. **Noah felt bad because he was TRYING to listen, but his brain kept going somewhere else. Have you felt that way?**

3. **Noah learned to check in with himself ("Am I still listening?") and doodle to help focus. What might help YOU notice when your mind wanders?**

TRY THIS!

This week, practice noticing when your mind wanders and bringing it back.

Your ADHD brain is like a puppy that wanders off to explore interesting things. You can't stop it completely, but you can learn to notice when it happens and call it back!

Try these tricks:

While listening in class or at home:

- Doodle on paper while listening (sounds weird, but it helps ADHD brains!)
- Take simple notes (even just a few words)
- Squeeze a stress ball or fidget with something quiet

Check in with yourself:

- Every few minutes, ask: "Am I still here? Am I listening?"
- If yes, great! Keep going
- If your mind wandered, that's okay! Just bring it back

While reading:

- Read a little bit, then stop
- Ask yourself: "What did I just read? Do I remember?"
- If you don't remember, your mind wandered! Read it again

At home (ask a parent to help):

- Set a timer to go off every 5 minutes while you work
- When it beeps, check: "Was I focused or was my mind wandering?"
- If wandering, bring it back
- Keep track: How many times did you catch your mind wandering?

Try this for one week. The goal isn't to NEVER let your mind wander. The goal is to NOTICE when it wanders so you can bring it back!

Remember: A wandering mind isn't bad. You're not in trouble. You're just practicing being a good "puppy trainer" for your brain!

Story 7: The Rush-and-Crash Kid

A story about learning that going slow helps you make fewer mistakes.

Sophie Anderson finished her math worksheet first! She always finished first.

She walked up to Mrs. Kim's desk and handed it in with a big smile.

"Great job finishing, Sophie," Mrs. Kim said. "But did you check your work?"

"Um... no."

Mrs. Kim looked at the first problem. "What's 4 + 5?"

"Nine!"

"So why did you write 8?"

Sophie looked at her paper. She HAD written 8! But she KNEW it was 9. "I made a mistake."

Mrs. Kim checked a few more problems. Sophie had gotten half of them wrong, but they were all problems she actually knew how to do. She'd just rushed and made careless mistakes.

"Sophie, you need to slow down and check your work."

"But I wanted to finish first!"

"Finishing first doesn't matter if you get it wrong. Quality is better than speed."

Sophie went back to her desk feeling frustrated. She HATED going slow. Slow felt impossible.

This was Sophie's biggest problem. She rushed through everything.

She'd speed through her homework making silly mistakes. She'd run in the hallway and crash into things. She'd start projects without reading the directions and do them wrong.

Yesterday, she'd tried to build a Lego set. The instructions said to start with the base, but Sophie just grabbed pieces and started building. When it didn't work, she got mad and gave up.

This morning, she'd gotten dressed so fast she'd put her shirt on backwards and inside out.

At lunch, she'd rushed to eat and spilled milk all over herself.

"Sophie, slow down!" her mom said at least ten times a day.

But Sophie's brain didn't DO slow. It only did FAST.

That weekend, Sophie's mom said, "Let's try something. We're going to have a 'turtle power' challenge."

"What's that?"

"Going slow on purpose. Like a turtle. We'll see if you can do one thing REALLY slow and careful."

"That sounds boring."

"Maybe. But let's try. Pick one thing to do turtle-slow today."

Sophie picked coloring a picture. She usually rushed through coloring, scribbling fast and going outside the lines.

This time, she went slow. Slow, careful coloring. Staying inside the lines. It felt WEIRD. Her brain wanted to go fast!

But when she finished, the picture looked really good. Way better than her fast coloring.

"See?" her mom said. "Slow can be good."

At school, Mrs. Kim gave Sophie a special challenge. "Today, I want you to do your math worksheet, but after EACH problem, check it. Don't do the whole page and then check. One problem, then check. Can you do that?"

Sophie nodded. It sounded slow and boring. But she'd try.

She did the first problem: $7 + 3 = 10$. She checked it. Yep, that was right!

She did the second problem: $5 + 6 = 11$. She checked it. Correct!

She kept going. One problem, then check. One problem, then check.

It took longer than usual. She didn't finish first. But when she turned it in, Mrs. Kim checked it and smiled. "Sophie! You got them ALL right! When you slowed down and checked, you didn't make careless mistakes."

Sophie felt proud. It was weird to not finish first. But getting them all right felt even better.

Sophie's mom helped her practice "turtle power" at home too.

When Sophie rushed to put on her shoes, her mom said, "Turtle power! Go slow and make sure they're on the right feet."

Sophie went slow. Left shoe, right foot. Right shoe, left foot. Perfect!

When Sophie rushed through reading, her mom said, "Turtle power! Read it slow enough to understand."

Sophie slowed down. She actually remembered what she read!

At first, going slow felt terrible. Sophie's brain wanted to rush. But the more she practiced, the easier it got. And she noticed she made way fewer mistakes when she used turtle power.

One day in art class, they were making paper airplanes. The teacher gave them instructions with six steps.

Old Sophie would have just started folding without reading. But New Sophie remembered: turtle power.

She read step 1 carefully. She did it. She checked it against the picture.

Then step 2. Carefully. Check.

Step 3. Careful. Check.

Other kids were already done, but their planes didn't look right. Sophie kept going slow and careful.

When she finished, her plane looked perfect! She threw it and it flew great!

The teacher said, "Sophie, yours came out so well! You followed the directions carefully."

Sophie felt proud. She hadn't finished first. But she'd done it RIGHT.

Sophie still liked going fast sometimes. At recess, she ran and played and went as fast as she wanted. That was good fast!

But she was learning when to use turtle power. For homework, for following directions, for checking her work. Those times, slow was better.

One day, her friend Olivia said, "How come you don't rush anymore?"

"I still rush sometimes. But I'm learning to slow down for important stuff. I call it turtle power."

"Does it work?"

"Yeah! I make way fewer mistakes now. Want to try?"

They practiced turtle power together, doing one math problem really slow and careful. Olivia liked it too!

At the end of second grade, Sophie's report card said she'd improved so much in checking her work and following directions.

That night, her mom said, "I'm so proud of you! You learned to use turtle power."

"I still like going fast."

"I know! And fast is okay sometimes. You just learned WHEN to go slow. That's important."

Sophie thought about the beginning of the year. She'd rushed through everything and made mistakes all the time. Her work was messy. She crashed into things. She got frustrated a lot.

Now she knew about turtle power. She could slow down when it mattered. She checked her work. She read directions. She still made mistakes sometimes, but way less than before.

That summer, Sophie got a new bike. She wanted to ride it right away!

But her dad said, "First, let's make sure it's adjusted right. Turtle power!"

Sophie laughed. "Okay, turtle power."

They slowly, carefully checked the seat height and the brakes. It took ten extra minutes.

But when Sophie rode her bike, it was perfect. And she didn't crash!

"See?" her dad said. "Sometimes slow is faster. You didn't have to stop and fix it later."

Sophie got it now. Rush, rush, rush made more work later when she had to fix mistakes. Turtle power meant doing it right the first time.

And doing it right felt really good.

THINK ABOUT IT

1. **Sophie rushed through everything and made lots of careless mistakes on things she actually knew how to do. Does this happen to you?** Do you go too fast and mess up?
2. **Sophie hated going slow because it felt boring. Do you feel that way too?** Does slow feel really hard?
3. **Sophie learned "turtle power" which meant going slow on purpose for important stuff. What could you try using turtle power on?** Homework? Getting dressed? Something else?

TRY THIS!

This week, try "turtle power" on one thing you usually rush through.

Your ADHD brain likes to go FAST. That's okay for some things! But for homework, following directions, and checking your work, slow is better.

Pick ONE thing to try turtle power on:
For homework:

- Do ONE problem, then check it
- Then do the next problem, then check it
- Don't rush ahead!

For following directions:

- Read step 1, do it, check it
- Then step 2, do it, check it
- Go step-by-step, slow and careful

For getting ready:

- Put on one piece of clothing at a time, nice and slow
- Check: Is it on right? Right foot? Not backwards?

Make it fun:

- Pretend you're a turtle moving slowly
- See if you can do it slower than normal (without being silly)
- Time yourself: Can you do it slow AND get it right?

After one week, notice:

- Did going slow help you make fewer mistakes?
- Did turtle power make your work better?
- Was it as boring as you thought, or actually kind of okay?

Remember: Fast isn't always better! Slow and RIGHT is better than fast and WRONG. You can still go fast at recess and play! But use turtle power for important stuff.

Story 8: The "I Can't Start" Problem

A story about learning that starting with one tiny step makes big tasks feel possible.

Marcus Johnson had a book report due in five days. He KNEW he had to do it. He WANTED to do it. But every time he sat down to start, he just... couldn't.

His brain felt stuck.

He'd sit at his desk with a blank paper. He'd stare at it. He'd think about the report. But he couldn't make himself START.

So he'd sharpen his pencil instead. Then he'd organize his desk. Then he'd get a snack. Then he'd check if his mom needed help with anything. Anything except actually starting the report.

"Marcus, have you started your book report?" his mom asked on Tuesday.

"I'm about to!"

But he wasn't. He sat at his desk again. Stared at the blank paper again. His brain felt frozen. He didn't know why!

Wednesday. Thursday. Still hadn't started. The report was due Monday. He was running out of time, but he STILL couldn't make himself start.

This happened with everything, not just book reports.

"Marcus, clean your room," his dad would say.

Marcus would look at his messy room. He needed to pick up toys, put away clothes, make his bed, organize his books. It all felt too BIG. He didn't know where to start. So he didn't start at all.

"Marcus, start your homework."

Marcus would look at the worksheet. Ten problems. That felt like a lot. He'd stare at it, unable to make himself begin.

People thought he was lazy or procrastinating on purpose. But Marcus wasn't being lazy! He genuinely didn't understand why he couldn't START things. It was like his brain was stuck in quicksand.

On Friday, with his book report due in three days, Marcus's mom said, "Let's talk to your teacher."

Mrs. Brown, his teacher, said, "Marcus, I know you have ADHD. Starting tasks is really hard for ADHD brains. Your brain sees the WHOLE big task and feels overwhelmed. We need to make the first step tiny."

"What do you mean?"

"Right now, you're thinking: I have to write a whole book report. That's big and scary. But what if you just think: I need to write the title of my book at the top of the paper. Can you do that?"

Marcus thought about it. Just writing the title? That didn't seem scary.

"Yeah, I can do that."

"Okay. Go do JUST that. Just the title. Nothing else."

Marcus went home. He sat at his desk. He wrote the title of his book at the top of the paper.

Done!

He went to tell his mom. "I wrote the title!"

"Great! Now put the paper away and take a break."

"But I should keep going..."

"Nope. You did the tiny step. That's enough for now."

An hour later, Marcus looked at the paper with the title on it. Now it didn't feel as scary. He'd already started!

"What's the next tiny step?" his mom asked.

"Um... write the author's name?"

"Perfect! Go do just that."

Marcus wrote the author's name. Done! Another tiny step.

Over the weekend, Marcus did his book report in tiny steps.

Saturday morning: Write one sentence about what the book is about.

Saturday afternoon: Write one sentence about his favorite character.

Sunday morning: Write one sentence about his favorite part.

Each tiny step felt doable. And once he did the tiny step, the next one felt easier.

By Sunday night, he'd finished the whole report! He hadn't done it all at once. He'd done it in lots of tiny steps. And it had worked!

Mrs. Brown taught the whole class about tiny steps.

"Sometimes big tasks feel overwhelming. The trick is to make the first step SO small that it's easy. Then once you've started, continuing is easier."

She gave them examples:

- Instead of "clean my room," think "pick up one toy"
- Instead of "do all my homework," think "do the first problem"
- Instead of "write a story," think "write one sentence"

Marcus tried it with homework. Instead of thinking about all ten math problems, he thought: Just do problem #1.

He did problem #1. That wasn't so bad!

Then: Just do problem #2.

Before he knew it, he'd done all ten problems. Starting with a tiny step had made the whole thing possible.

At home, Marcus used tiny steps for cleaning his room.

His room was messy. Clothes on the floor, toys everywhere, bed unmade. Looking at it all felt overwhelming.

But he thought: Just pick up one shirt.

He picked up one shirt and put it in the hamper.

Then: Just pick up one toy.

He picked up one toy and put it on the shelf.

He kept doing tiny steps. After twenty minutes, his whole room was clean! He'd done it by breaking it into pieces so small they didn't feel scary.

One day, his friend Jayden said, "How come you're getting your homework done now? At the beginning of the year, you never did it."

"I learned about tiny steps. Instead of trying to do the whole thing, I just do the first tiny step. Then the next tiny step. It makes it feel less scary."

"I should try that. Sometimes I can't start stuff either."

"Yeah! Like right now, we're supposed to start reading. Don't think about reading the whole chapter. Just think: read the first paragraph. That's it."

Jayden tried it. He read the first paragraph. Then the next. Then the next.

"Hey, it worked!" Jayden said. "I'm actually reading and I didn't even feel stuck!"

Marcus's grandma came to visit. She saw him doing homework.

"You're so focused!" she said.

"I'm using tiny steps. See, I'm not thinking about all the homework. I'm just thinking: do this one problem. Then this one problem. It helps me not feel stuck."

"That's very smart."

"My brain has trouble starting big things. But tiny things are easy!"

That night, his grandma needed to write a long email. She said, "I don't want to do this. It's going to take forever."

Marcus said, "Use tiny steps, Grandma! Just write one sentence. Then another sentence."

His grandma laughed. "You're right!" She wrote one sentence. Then another. After a few minutes, the email was done.

"Thank you for teaching me tiny steps, Marcus!"

Marcus felt proud. His strategy worked for other people too!

At the end of the year, Marcus's report card said he'd improved SO much in completing his work on time.

His mom hugged him. "You figured it out!"

"I still have trouble starting sometimes. But now I know what to do. Tiny steps!"

"That's a strategy you'll use your whole life."

That summer, Marcus wanted to build a huge Lego castle. Looking at all the pieces felt overwhelming.

But he remembered: tiny steps. Just build one wall. That's it.

He built one wall. Then thought: just add one tower.

He added one tower.

He kept going, one tiny step at a time. After a few days, the whole castle was done!

His little sister said, "Wow! How did you build something so big?"

"Tiny steps. I didn't try to build it all at once. I did one little piece, then another little piece. Eventually, all the little pieces made something big!"

And that was the secret. Big things were just lots of tiny steps put together.

Starting felt impossible when you thought about the whole thing. But starting felt easy when you just thought about the first tiny step.

Marcus's brain still got stuck sometimes. But now he knew what to do.

Just start with something tiny.

And then do the next tiny thing.

And the next.

And before he knew it, the big thing would be done.

THINK ABOUT IT

1. **Marcus knew he needed to do his book report but he couldn't make himself start. Does this**

happen to you? Do you ever feel stuck and unable to begin even when you want to?

2. **Marcus would do other things (sharpen pencils, get snacks, organize his desk) instead of starting. Do you do this too?** What do you do instead of starting?

3. **Marcus learned to make the first step SO tiny it didn't feel scary (like just writing the title). What big thing could YOU break into tiny steps?**

TRY THIS!

This week, practice starting with one tiny step.

Your ADHD brain gets stuck when tasks feel big. But tiny steps feel easy! Once you start, continuing is easier.

Here's how to use tiny steps:

For homework:

- Don't think: "I have to do all this homework"
- Instead think: "I just need to write my name and date"
- Do that tiny step
- Then think: "I just need to do problem #1"
- Do that tiny step
- Keep going one tiny step at a time

For cleaning your room:

- Don't think: "I have to clean this whole mess"
- Instead think: "I just need to pick up one thing"
- Pick up one thing
- Then: "Pick up one more thing"
- Keep going with tiny steps

For big projects:

- Break it into the tiniest first step possible
- Example: Book report? Tiny step = write the title
- Example: Art project? Tiny step = get out the materials
- Example: Reading? Tiny step = read one paragraph

Ask a parent to help you:

- When you feel stuck, ask: "What's the tiniest first step?"
- Do JUST that tiny step
- Celebrate! You started!
- Then do the next tiny step

Try this for one week. Notice: Is starting easier when you make the first step tiny?

Remember: You're not lazy! Your brain just needs tiny steps to get unstuck. Once you start, the rest gets easier!

STORY 9: THE LOSE-EVERYTHING KID

A story about learning that when you always lose things, you need special spots where things always go.

Aisha Brown couldn't find her homework. Again.

"I HAD it!" she told her teacher, Ms. Garcia. "I did it last night! I put it in my backpack!"

Ms. Garcia had heard this before. "Aisha, can you check your backpack one more time?"

Aisha dumped everything out. Books, papers, a broken crayon, a snack wrapper from last week, crumpled papers. No homework.

She found it later that day stuffed inside her math book. But by then, it was too late to turn in.

This was Aisha's life. She lost everything. Her jacket, her lunch box, her pencils, her homework, her library books. If it could be lost, Aisha lost it.

"Where's your jacket?" her mom asked after school.

"I don't know! I had it at recess..."

They found it on the playground. Again.

"Aisha, you need to keep track of your things!"

But Aisha didn't know HOW. Things just... disappeared.

At home, Aisha's room was a disaster. Clothes on the floor mixed with toys mixed with books mixed with art supplies. Everything jumbled together.

"Time to do homework," her mom said.

"I can't find a pencil!"

"You had three pencils yesterday!"

"I know, but I don't know where they are!"

They searched through the mess and found one pencil under her bed.

"Where's your math worksheet?"

"In my backpack."

But when Aisha looked in her backpack, the worksheet wasn't there. They searched for ten minutes. Finally found it in the kitchen. How did it get there? Aisha had no idea.

By the time they found everything, Aisha was frustrated and tired. And homework hadn't even started yet!

Aisha's dad sat with her that weekend. "We need to make a system. Your ADHD brain doesn't keep track of where things are. So we need special spots where things ALWAYS go. Every single time. No exceptions."

"But I try to put things away!"

"I know. But 'away' is too vague. We need EXACT spots. Watch."

They got a hook by the door and put a sign under it that said JACKET. "Your jacket always goes on this hook. Every time you come home. Always."

They got a basket by the door with a sign that said BACK-PACK. "Your backpack always goes in this basket. Every time. Always."

They got a pencil box for Aisha's desk. "Pencils ALWAYS go in this box. Nowhere else. If you use a pencil, it goes back in this box."

They cleared a spot on her desk and put a sign that said

HOMEWORK. "Finished homework ALWAYS goes here until you put it in your backpack in the morning."

"But what if I forget?" Aisha asked.

"We'll make reminders. Like, when you walk in the door, the first thing you do is put your jacket on the hook and your backpack in the basket. Before you do ANYTHING else. We'll practice until it's automatic."

They practiced. Aisha walked in the door. Put jacket on hook. Put backpack in basket.

"Good! Now go outside and do it again."

Aisha went outside and came back in. Jacket on hook. Backpack in basket.

They practiced ten times until it felt natural.

Her dad also helped her clean her room using the "home spots" method. Every single thing needed its own home.

"Books go on the shelf. Always. Toys go in this bin. Always. Clothes go in the hamper or dresser. Always."

They spent all Saturday cleaning and organizing. Everything got a home. Then they took pictures of what each spot should look like and taped the pictures on the wall as reminders.

The first week was hard. On Monday, Aisha came home and started to walk to the kitchen.

"Aisha! What are you forgetting?" her mom called.

"Oh!" Aisha went back. Jacket on hook. Backpack in basket.

On Tuesday, she did her homework but left it on her desk instead of putting it in the homework spot.

The next morning, she couldn't find it. "Where's my homework?!"

Her mom helped her look. It was on her desk, but not in the homework spot. It had gotten mixed with other papers.

"Remember, finished homework goes in the homework spot. Let's put it there now so you know where it is tomorrow."

On Wednesday, Aisha remembered! She came home. Jacket on hook. Backpack in basket. Did homework. Put finished homework in the homework spot. In the morning, she knew exactly where it was!

"You did it!" her mom said.

At school, Ms. Garcia helped Aisha make a system too.

Aisha got a special folder for homework. It was bright yellow so it was easy to spot. "Homework from school goes in this folder right away. When you finish it at home, it goes back in this folder. The folder stays in your backpack. Always."

Aisha also got a pencil pouch that attached to her backpack. "Pencils go in this pouch. Nowhere else."

And she got a special spot in her cubby for her jacket with her name on it. "Jacket goes here. Every time."

Ms. Garcia also gave Aisha a checklist for the end of the day:

- Homework in yellow folder? Check!

- Yellow folder in backpack? Check!
- Pencil pouch in backpack? Check!
- Jacket in cubby or on me? Check!

Every day before going home, Aisha used the checklist. At first, she forgot things on the checklist. But the more she used it, the better she got.

After a few weeks, Aisha's systems were working!

She came home. Jacket on hook. Backpack in basket. Every single day. It became automatic.

She did homework. Put it in the homework spot. Every time.

She used a pencil. Put it back in the pencil box. Every time.

One day, her friend Hannah came over. "Wow, your room is so organized now!"

"Yeah, everything has a home. See? Books go here, toys go here, art stuff goes here. If everything has a home, I can find it."

"I lose stuff all the time too. Can you show me?"

Aisha showed Hannah how to give everything a home spot. "The trick is it has to be the SAME spot every single time. Not just 'put it away.' But 'put it in this exact spot.'"

Aisha still lost things sometimes. One day she couldn't find her library book. She looked in her room. Not there. Looked in her backpack. Not there.

But then she remembered her system. "Where does my library book go?"

There was a basket by her bed labeled LIBRARY BOOKS. She checked there.

Found it!

Another time, she thought she'd lost her homework folder. But she remembered: the folder goes in the backpack. She checked. There it was!

The systems worked because they told her brain exactly where to look. Instead of searching everywhere, she only had to check the home spots.

At parent-teacher conferences, Ms. Garcia said, "Aisha has improved so much! She's not losing things nearly as often."

"We made systems," Aisha explained. "Everything has a home. I don't have to remember where I put something because it ALWAYS goes in the same spot."

"That's very smart," Ms. Garcia said.

"My ADHD brain forgets where I put things. But if things always go in the same spot, I don't have to remember. The spot remembers for me!"

At the end of the year, Aisha only lost her jacket twice (compared to three times a week at the beginning!). She turned in her homework almost every day. She could find her pencils. She didn't lose library books.

Her mom was amazed. "Remember at the beginning of the year when we were searching for lost things every single day?"

"I know! Now I know where everything is. Well, mostly."

"The systems really work."

That summer, Aisha went to her grandma's house for a week. On the first day, she set up her systems there.

Jacket on this chair by the door. Always.

Backpack in this corner. Always.

Her stuff in this drawer. Always.

Her grandma said, "You're so organized!"

"I have ADHD so I lose things a lot. But if everything has one home, I can find it. Want me to help you organize your kitchen?"

They spent the afternoon giving everything in grandma's kitchen a home spot. Measuring cups in this drawer. Always. Spoons in this container. Always.

"This is wonderful!" her grandma said. "I can find everything now!"

Aisha smiled. Her ADHD brain didn't naturally keep track of where things were. But her systems did it for her.

Everything had a home. And as long as things went back to their homes, she could always find them.

THINK ABOUT IT

1. **Aisha lost things constantly because her ADHD brain didn't keep track of where she put stuff. Do you lose things a lot too?** What do you lose most?
2. **Aisha learned that everything needs one exact home spot, not just "put it away somewhere." Does having exact spots for things help you, or do you forget where the spots are?**
3. **Aisha's systems helped her find things because she only had to check the home spots. What things do YOU lose most that need home spots?**

TRY THIS!

This week, make home spots for the things you lose most.

Your ADHD brain doesn't remember where you put things. So instead of trying to remember, make EXACT spots where things ALWAYS go!

Pick 3 things you lose most often. Give each one a home:

Example homes:

- Jacket: Hook by the door (ALWAYS)
- Backpack: Basket by the door (ALWAYS)
- Homework: Folder in backpack (ALWAYS)
- Pencils: Pencil box on desk (ALWAYS)
- Shoes: Mat by the door (ALWAYS)

Make it work (ask a parent to help):

- Put a label or sign at each home spot
- Practice using the spots for one week
- Every time you use something, it goes back to its home RIGHT AWAY
- Not later. Not "I'll put it away after." Right away!

Make reminders:

- Put a checklist by the door: "Jacket on hook? Backpack in basket?"

- Use it every day when you come home and before you leave

After one week, check:

- Are you losing things less?
- Can you find your stuff faster?
- Do you spend less time searching?

Remember: Your brain doesn't remember where things are. But home spots remember FOR you! You just have to put things in their homes every time!

Story 10: The Homework Battle

A story about learning that homework is easier when you break it into chunks and remove distractions.

Tyler Chen hated homework time. Every single day, it was a battle.

"Time for homework, Tyler," his mom said.

Tyler groaned. He sat at the kitchen table with his worksheet. He picked up his pencil. He looked at the first problem.

Then he looked out the window. Then he tapped his pencil. Then he got up to get water. Then he came back and stared at the paper some more.

Thirty minutes later, he still hadn't done a single problem.

"Tyler! You haven't even started!" his mom said, frustrated.

"I'm trying!"

But he wasn't, really. Or he was trying, but his brain wouldn't cooperate. Homework felt SO hard and SO boring. He just couldn't make himself do it.

This happened every day. Homework that should take twenty minutes took two hours. And most of that time was just sitting there not doing it.

By the time Tyler finally finished his homework, he was tired and grumpy. He'd missed playing outside. He'd missed his favorite show. All because homework took FOREVER.

"Why is homework so hard for you?" his dad asked. "You're smart! You can do this stuff."

"I don't know! I just can't make myself do it."

The truth was, when Tyler sat down to do homework, everything else suddenly seemed more interesting. The sounds outside. The TV in the other room. His own thoughts about video games. Anything was better than homework.

And when he DID try to focus, the homework felt overwhelming. Ten math problems? That felt like a mountain. A whole page of reading? Impossible.

So he'd sit there, frozen, doing nothing.

Tyler's parents talked to his teacher, Mr. Lopez.

"Tyler has ADHD," Mr. Lopez explained. "Homework is extra hard for ADHD kids. Sitting still, focusing, starting tasks, staying on task... homework requires all the things ADHD brains struggle with."

"So what do we do?" Tyler's mom asked.

"We make it easier. Break homework into tiny chunks. Remove distractions. Give breaks. Make it feel less overwhelming."

That night, Tyler's parents tried a new approach.

Instead of "do your homework," they said, "Let's do just five problems. That's it."

Five problems didn't sound that bad. Tyler did five problems.

"Great! Now take a five-minute break. Go run around outside."

Tyler ran outside, played, came back.

"Okay, five more problems."

He did five more. Another break. Five more problems. Another break.

Before he knew it, all the homework was done! And it hadn't felt as terrible because he got breaks and it was in small chunks.

Tyler's dad also helped him make a better homework space.

They moved his homework spot away from the window so Tyler couldn't see outside. They turned off the TV. They put his phone in another room.

"Your ADHD brain gets distracted by everything," his dad explained. "So we're removing distractions before you start."

They also made a "homework time" rule. For the first ten minutes, Tyler had to do homework. No getting up, no water, no bathroom. Just ten minutes of work.

"I can't do homework for ten whole minutes!" Tyler said.

"Try. Just ten. If you really can't after ten minutes, we'll take a break."

Tyler tried. He set a timer for ten minutes and worked. It was hard! His brain wanted to wander. His body wanted to move. But he kept working.

When the timer beeped, he'd done three problems!

"See? You CAN do it for ten minutes. Now take a three-minute break."

Tyler ran in place, did jumping jacks, got water. Then another ten minutes of work.

The new system was:

- Homework in a spot with no distractions
- Work for ten minutes
- Break for three minutes
- Work for ten minutes
- Break for three minutes
- Keep going until done

Some days, Tyler could work for fifteen minutes before needing a break. Some days, ten minutes was all he could handle. But either way, he was getting homework done way faster than before!

At school, Mr. Lopez helped too. He gave Tyler his homework sheet at the beginning of the day instead of the end.

"If you finish your classwork early, you can start homework. Then you'll have less to do at home."

Tyler started using extra time at school to get ahead on homework. If he could do even two problems at school, that was two fewer to do at home!

After a few weeks, homework battles were way less intense.

Tyler came home. Snack first, then homework.

He went to his homework spot (no TV, no window, no distractions).

He set the timer for ten minutes. He worked.

Timer beeps. Break! He ran around, got water, moved his body.

Timer for ten more minutes. He worked.

Some days, homework still took a while. But it wasn't taking two hours anymore. More like forty minutes. And that forty minutes had breaks, so it felt less horrible.

One day, his friend Alex came over. "Want to play?"

"I have to finish homework first. But it only takes like ten more minutes."

"Only ten minutes? My homework takes forever!"

"I break it into chunks. Ten minutes of work, then a short break. Want to try it together?"

They did homework together using Tyler's system. Ten minutes work, three minutes break. Ten minutes work, three minutes break.

"This is way better!" Alex said. "I usually just sit there forever not doing anything. This actually works!"

Tyler's mom noticed something else. Tyler was less grumpy in the evenings.

"You seem happier lately."

"Homework doesn't take all night anymore. I actually have time to play!"

Before, homework dragged on so long that by the time he finished, it was bedtime. He never got to play or relax. Now, he finished homework faster and had time for fun stuff.

His dad was proud. "You figured out how to work WITH your ADHD brain instead of against it."

"What do you mean?"

"Your brain needs breaks and movement. Fighting that made homework horrible. But giving your brain what it needs, breaks and chunks, made homework actually doable."

At the end of the year, Mr. Lopez said Tyler had improved so much in completing homework.

"I break it into chunks," Tyler explained. "My ADHD brain

can't do homework for an hour straight. But it CAN do ten minutes. So I do ten minutes, break, ten minutes, break. Eventually it's all done!"

That summer, Tyler had summer reading. Five books! That sounded like SO much.

But he remembered his system. He didn't try to read a whole book at once. He read for fifteen minutes, then took a break. Read for fifteen minutes, break.

Little by little, he got through all five books. Not by forcing himself to read for hours, but by doing small chunks with breaks.

His little sister watched him. "How come you can focus on reading?"

"I can't focus for a long time. But I can focus for fifteen minutes. So that's what I do. Fifteen minutes, break, fifteen minutes, break."

"Can I try that for my homework?"

"Yeah! It makes it way less awful."

And it did. Homework was still homework. It wasn't fun. But it didn't have to be a two-hour battle anymore.

Tyler's ADHD brain needed breaks and chunks and no distractions. When he gave his brain what it needed, homework became doable.

Not easy. But doable.

And that was good enough.

THINK ABOUT IT

1. **Tyler sat down to do homework but couldn't make himself start, and it took forever. Does homework feel like a battle for you too?** What makes it so hard?
2. **Tyler's brain got distracted by everything (TV, window, his own thoughts). What distracts YOU most during homework?**
3. **Tyler learned to break homework into ten-minute chunks with breaks. Do you think this would help you, or would you need different chunks (shorter? longer?)?**

TRY THIS!

This week, try the "chunk and break" method for homework.

Your ADHD brain can't focus for a long time. But it CAN focus for short chunks! Work for a short time, then break, then work again.

Set up for success (ask a parent to help):
Remove distractions BEFORE starting:

- Turn off TV
- Put phone in another room
- Sit away from windows
- No toys or games nearby

Use the chunk and break system:

- Set a timer for 10 minutes
- Work the whole time (no getting up!)
- When timer beeps, take a 3-minute break
- Do something active: run, jump, dance, get water
- Then do another 10 minutes

Keep going: 10 minutes work, 3 minutes break, 10 minutes work, 3 minutes break, until homework is done

Adjust if needed:

- If 10 minutes is too long, try 7 minutes
- If you can do 15 minutes, great!
- Find what works for YOUR brain

Try this for one week. Track your time: Does homework take less time with this method?

Remember: You're not lazy! Your ADHD brain just needs breaks and chunks. Give it what it needs and homework gets easier!

Story 11: The Friend Trouble

A story about learning that ADHD can make friendships

tricky, but you can learn to notice and fix friendship problems.

Maya Patel didn't understand why kids got mad at her.

At recess, she was playing tag with some girls. She was having SO much fun! She tagged Sophia really hard.

"Ow! Maya, that hurt!" Sophia said.

"Sorry! I was just excited!"

"You always play too rough," Sophia said. The other girls walked away.

Maya felt confused and sad. She didn't mean to play rough. She just got really excited and couldn't control how hard she tagged.

This happened a lot. Maya would get too excited and be too loud or too rough. Or she'd interrupt people when they were talking. Or she'd talk about the same thing (horses!) for way too long and other kids would get bored.

She didn't mean to annoy people. But somehow, she kept doing it.

At lunch, Maya sat with Emma and Lily. Emma was telling a story about her weekend.

"And then we went to the beach and..."

"I LOVE the beach!" Maya interrupted. "One time at the beach I found a shell and it was so cool and I collected like fifty shells and..."

Emma stopped talking. She looked annoyed.

"I wasn't done with my story," Emma said quietly.

"Oh. Sorry." Maya felt bad. She'd interrupted again.

Later, Maya wanted to tell them about her favorite horse breed. She talked and talked about horses. After a few minutes, Emma and Lily looked bored.

"Can we talk about something else?" Lily asked.

Maya felt hurt. Didn't they care about what she liked?

But she also noticed: she'd been talking about horses for ten whole minutes and hadn't let them say anything.

That night, Maya cried to her mom. "Nobody wants to be my friend! They say I'm annoying!"

"Oh honey, you're not annoying. But your ADHD does make friendships trickier."

"How?"

"ADHD makes you interrupt without meaning to. It makes you talk a lot about your interests and not notice when others are bored. It makes you get too excited and play too rough. You're not trying to be rude. Your ADHD brain just makes it harder to notice social stuff."

"So I'll never have friends?"

"No! You can learn strategies. You can practice noticing when people are getting annoyed and adjusting. Let me show you."

Maya's mom taught her some friendship skills.

For interrupting: "Before you talk, count to three and make sure the other person is done. If you have a thought, hold it in your brain for three seconds. It won't disappear."

For talking too much about one thing: "Use a timer. Talk about your interest for two minutes, then ask the other person a question about THEIR interest. Back and forth."

For playing too rough: "When you get excited, your body gets wild. Before you tag someone or hug them, stop and ask yourself: gentle or rough? Then choose gentle."

For noticing when people are annoyed: "Watch their faces and bodies. Are they looking away? Backing up? Sounding frustrated? Those are clues they're getting annoyed."

Maya practiced with her mom. They pretended to have conversations. Maya practiced not interrupting, taking turns talking, and noticing body language.

At school, Maya tried her new skills.

At lunch, Emma was talking. Maya opened her mouth to interrupt.

Wait. Count to three. Is she done talking?

No, she's still talking.

Maya waited. Emma finished her story. THEN Maya talked.

"Thanks for waiting," Emma said. "You usually interrupt."

"I'm practicing!"

Later, Maya wanted to talk about horses. She talked for two

minutes (her mom had helped her practice what two minutes felt like). Then she stopped.

"Lily, what did you do this weekend?"

Lily looked surprised. Usually Maya just talked and talked. "Oh! I went to my cousin's house."

They had a real conversation! Back and forth. Not just Maya talking.

At recess, they played tag again. Maya felt SUPER excited. She wanted to tag Sophia really hard!

But she stopped herself. Gentle or rough? Choose gentle.

She tagged Sophia gently.

"Thanks for not tagging hard!" Sophia said.

Maya felt proud. She'd remembered!

Sophia noticed something else too. "You've been better at not interrupting lately."

"Really?"

"Yeah! At the beginning of the year, you interrupted all the time. Now you wait. It's nice."

Maya felt so happy. People were noticing!

Maya still made mistakes. One day, she got really excited and talked about horses for way too long. She noticed Emma's face looking bored.

Oh no. She'd done it again.

"Sorry, I'm talking about horses too much, aren't I?"

Emma nodded.

"Okay, I'll stop. What do you want to talk about?"

Emma smiled. "Thanks for noticing."

Another time, Maya accidentally interrupted. But instead of just keeping talking, she caught herself.

"Oh sorry, I interrupted. What were you saying?"

The other girl said, "It's okay. I was just saying that..."

Maya waited and listened.

Maya's teacher, Mrs. Johnson, helped her practice friendship skills at school too.

Before recess, Mrs. Johnson would remind Maya: "Remember, gentle tagging. Watch faces to see if people are having fun or getting annoyed."

After recess, Mrs. Johnson would check in. "How did it go?"

"Good! I played tag and I remembered to tag gently. And I noticed when kids were done playing and wanted to do something else, so I didn't force them to keep playing."

"That's great awareness, Maya!"

Mrs. Johnson also helped Maya practice conversations. "Talk for one minute about your interest, then ask your friend a question. Back and forth. That's how conversations work."

After a few months, Maya had more friends. Not because she changed who she was, but because she learned skills to help her ADHD brain notice social stuff better.

She still interrupted sometimes, but way less. And when she did, she'd catch herself and apologize.

She still got really excited, but she'd learned to check: gentle or rough? And choose gentle.

She still loved talking about horses, but she learned to take turns. Talk for a bit, then ask the other person about their interests.

She still made mistakes. But she was getting better.

One day, a new girl named Zara joined their class. Maya noticed Zara sitting alone at lunch.

Maya sat with her. "Hi! I'm Maya. Want to sit with me and my friends?"

"Sure," Zara said quietly.

Maya introduced her to Emma and Lily. They all ate lunch together.

Later, Zara said, "Thanks for including me. I was nervous about being new."

"No problem! I know how it feels when friendship stuff is hard."

At the end of the year, Maya's mom asked, "Do you still think nobody wants to be your friend?"

"No! I have friends now. Emma, Lily, Sophia, and Zara."

"What changed?"

"I learned skills. Like not interrupting, taking turns in conversations, playing gently, and noticing when people are annoyed. My ADHD makes friendship harder, but I can learn strategies that help."

"I'm so proud of you."

That summer, Maya invited Emma over to play. They took turns talking about horses (Maya's interest) and art (Emma's interest).

Maya's mom watched them playing nicely together and smiled.

Maya's ADHD still made friendships take more work. She

had to pay attention to things other kids did automatically. She had to practice skills other kids didn't need to practice.

But she could do it. And she was doing it.

She had friends. Real friends.

And that felt really, really good.

THINK ABOUT IT

1. **Maya interrupted people, talked too much about her interests, and played too rough without meaning to. Do you sometimes annoy people without trying to?** What happens?

2. **Maya didn't notice when people were getting annoyed until her mom taught her to watch faces and body language. Is it hard for you to notice how other people are feeling?**

3. **Maya learned skills like counting to three before talking, taking turns in conversations, and choosing "gentle" when excited. Which of these might help YOU with friendships?**

TRY THIS!

This week, practice one friendship skill.

ADHD can make friendships tricky because it's harder to notice social stuff. But you can learn skills that help!

Pick ONE skill to practice this week:

Skill 1: Don't interrupt

- When someone is talking, count to 3 before you talk
- Make sure they're done before you start
- If you interrupt, say "Sorry!" and let them finish

Skill 2: Take turns talking

- Talk about YOUR interest for 2 minutes
- Then ask: "What do YOU like?" or "What did YOU do?"
- Let them talk for 2 minutes
- Back and forth!

Skill 3: Gentle, not rough

- When you get excited, your body gets wild
- Before you tag, hug, or touch someone, think: gentle or rough?
- Choose gentle!

Skill 4: Notice when people are annoyed

- Watch faces: Are they looking away? Frowning?
- Listen to voices: Do they sound frustrated?
- Watch bodies: Are they backing up or leaving?

- If yes, stop what you're doing and ask: "Are you okay?"

Practice with family first:

- Ask a parent or sibling to help you practice
- They can tell you when you interrupt or talk too long
- Practice makes it easier!

Try ONE skill for a whole week. Notice: Do friends seem happier? Do you get in less friendship trouble?

Remember: ADHD makes friendships harder. But you can learn skills! It takes practice, but it's worth it!

Story 12: The Good-At-This Kid

A story about learning that ADHD brains are good at some things, not just bad at others.

Diego Martinez was terrible at sitting still. Terrible at remembering things. Terrible at focusing on boring stuff.

He knew all the things his ADHD made hard. Everyone reminded him every day.

"Diego, sit still!" at school. "Diego, you forgot again!" at home. "Diego, pay attention!" everywhere.

He felt like ADHD was only bad things. Only problems. Only stuff he couldn't do.

Until art class.

In art class, Mrs. Franklin said, "Today, make something creative. Anything you want. You have one hour."

Some kids didn't know what to make. They sat there thinking.

But Diego's brain exploded with ideas! He could make a robot! No wait, a castle! No, a rocket ship that's also a castle! With dragons! And astronauts!

His hands started building before he even had a full plan. He grabbed cardboard, tape, markers, pipe cleaners. He built and created and added things.

His brain jumped from idea to idea, but that was GOOD in art! Each new idea made his project cooler!

Before he knew it, he'd made an amazing space-castle-dragon-robot. It was wild and creative and unlike anything anyone else made.

"Diego, this is incredible!" Mrs. Franklin said. "You have such a creative mind!"

Diego felt surprised. His jumping-around brain was GOOD at something?

That weekend, Diego's family went hiking. His older sister complained the whole time. "This is boring. When are we done?"

But Diego noticed EVERYTHING. A cool mushroom! Weird bark on that tree! A lizard! Birds making a nest! A stream with tiny fish!

"Diego, you see things nobody else sees," his dad said. "You notice details."

Diego thought about it. His ADHD brain that got distracted by everything during homework... that same brain noticed amazing things on hikes.

At home, Diego's abuela (grandma) was looking for her glasses. Everyone searched. Nobody could find them.

Diego walked into the room and immediately spotted them on top of the bookshelf, partially hidden behind a plant.

"How did you see those?" his mom asked. "We all looked!"

"I don't know, I just notice stuff."

His ADHD brain that noticed EVERYTHING and got distracted easily? That same brain was really good at spotting things other people missed.

On Monday, something scary happened at school. There was a fire drill, but it was a surprise and the alarm was really loud.

Some kids froze. Some kids panicked. The teacher was trying to get everyone calm and lined up.

Diego's brain went into emergency mode. He thought fast. He helped the kid next to him who was covering his ears. He grabbed the class bunny's cage so they wouldn't forget the bunny. He held the door for everyone.

Later, the teacher said, "Diego, you handled that really well. You stayed calm and helped others."

Diego's mom picked him up and the teacher told her about it. "Diego thinks quickly in unexpected situations. His ability to switch focus rapidly was actually helpful today."

Diego thought about that. His ADHD brain that jumped from thing to thing and couldn't stick with one task? In an emergency, that same brain could think fast and handle multiple things at once.

That week, Diego's class did a group project. They had to build a bridge out of straws.

Some kids wanted to plan everything perfectly before starting. They drew diagrams. They discussed. They thought and thought.

Diego's brain didn't work that way. He wanted to just TRY stuff. "Let's build something and see if it works!"

"But we need a plan!" the other kids said.

"We can change the plan as we go! Let's just try!"

They tried Diego's approach. They built a bridge. It fell down. They changed it. Built it again. Fell down again. Changed it more. Tried again.

After trying five different ways, they found one that worked!

Later, the teacher said, "Some people plan first, then build. Some people build first, then adjust. Diego's group used the try-and-adjust method and it worked great! Different approaches are valuable."

Diego realized: his ADHD brain that jumped into things without planning? That was good for trying new stuff and not being afraid of failure.

At home, Diego asked his parents, "Is ADHD all bad? Or is some of it good?"

His dad thought about it. "ADHD makes some things harder. Sitting still, remembering, focusing on boring stuff.

Those are real challenges. But ADHD also gives your brain some superpowers."

"Like what?"

"Like creativity. Your brain makes connections other people don't see. Like noticing details. You spot things others miss. Like thinking fast in surprises. Your brain switches gears quickly. Like trying new approaches. You're not afraid to experiment."

"Really?"

"Really. ADHD isn't all good or all bad. It's both. The trick is learning to work with what your brain does well."

Diego's mom added, "You're not broken. You're different. And different has strengths."

Diego started noticing his ADHD strengths more.

In art, his creative brain came up with amazing ideas.

On hikes, his noticing brain saw cool things.

When his friend lost his toy, Diego's detail-spotting brain found it in seconds.

When plans changed suddenly, Diego's fast-thinking brain adapted quickly.

When projects seemed impossible, Diego's try-stuff brain experimented until something worked.

Yes, ADHD made things hard. Homework was still a battle. Sitting still was still hard. Remembering was still tough.

But ADHD also made things easier. Creating. Noticing. Fast thinking. Trying new things. Adapting.

One day, a kid in class said, "I wish I didn't have ADHD. It makes everything hard."

Diego said, "It does make some stuff hard. But it makes other stuff easier. Like, I'm really creative. I notice things other people don't. I think fast when things change. Those are my ADHD superpowers."

"Really? ADHD has good parts?"

"Yeah! The jumping-around brain that makes homework hard? That same brain comes up with cool ideas in art. The noticing-everything brain that gets distracted? That same brain spots details others miss. It's the same brain, just different situations."

The other kid thought about that. "I never thought of it that way."

"Me neither! But it's true. ADHD isn't all bad. You just have to find what your ADHD brain is good at."

At the end of the year, Diego got an award in art class for "Most Creative Projects."

He also got picked to help with school tours because he noticed when new kids looked nervous and helped them feel welcome.

And his teacher mentioned in his report card that Diego had "excellent creative problem-solving skills and adapts well to change."

That night, Diego's family celebrated.

"I'm proud of you," his dad said. "Not just for the award. But for learning to see your strengths."

"ADHD still makes stuff hard," Diego said. "I still struggle with homework and sitting still and remembering."

"I know. Those challenges are real. But so are your strengths. You're creative, observant, fast-thinking, and adaptable. That's not despite ADHD. That's part of how your brain works."

Diego smiled. For so long, he'd only heard about ADHD problems. ADHD made him bad at this, bad at that.

But now he knew: ADHD also made him GOOD at things. Really good.

He wasn't broken. He was different.

And different had value.

THINK ABOUT IT

1. **Diego thought ADHD was only problems until he realized his ADHD brain was also good at creativity, noticing details, and thinking fast. What is YOUR ADHD brain good at?**

2. **The same brain that made homework hard helped Diego in art and emergencies. Have you noticed your brain working really well in some situations but not others?** When does your brain work best?

3. **Diego learned that he's not broken, just different. Do you sometimes feel broken because ADHD makes things hard?** How does it feel to know ADHD also has strengths?

TRY THIS!

This week, find ONE thing your ADHD brain is good at.

ADHD makes some things hard. That's true! But ADHD also makes some things easier. Your brain has strengths!

ADHD superpowers to look for:

Creativity:

- Do you come up with lots of ideas?
- Are you good at art, building, or making up stories?
- Do you think of solutions other people don't think of?

Noticing details:

- Do you spot things others miss?
- Are you good at finding lost things?
- Do you notice cool stuff in nature or around you?

Fast thinking:

- When things change suddenly, can you adapt quickly?
- Are you good in emergencies or surprises?
- Can your brain switch topics fast?

Trying new things:

- Are you brave about experimenting?
- Do you like to just TRY stuff instead of planning forever?
- Are you okay with failing and trying again?

Passion and energy:

- When you like something, do you REALLY like it?
- Can you focus super hard on things you love?
- Do you have lots of energy for fun stuff?

This week:

- Notice when your brain works really WELL
- What were you doing?
- How did your ADHD brain help?
- Tell someone: "My ADHD brain is good at ________!"

Make a list:

- Ask parents/teachers: "What am I good at?"
- Write down your ADHD strengths
- When ADHD feels hard, remember: your brain has superpowers too!

Remember: ADHD makes some stuff hard. But it also makes you creative, observant, fast-thinking, passionate, and unique. You're not broken. You're different. And different is valuable!

WHAT IS ADHD?

A Simple Explanation for Kids

What does ADHD stand for?

ADHD stands for Attention-Deficit/Hyperactivity Disorder. That's a big name! But what it really means is that your brain works differently than some other kids' brains.

What is ADHD?

ADHD is the way your brain is built. It's not something you catch like a cold. It's not something that goes away. You were born with an ADHD brain, and you'll have it your whole life.

Think of it like this: some people have brown eyes, some have blue eyes. Some people have ADHD brains, some don't. It's just a difference in how brains work!

How is an ADHD brain different?

ADHD brains work in special ways:

Attention: Your brain might have trouble focusing on boring stuff (like homework), but can super-focus on interesting stuff (like video games or building or drawing). Your brain decides what's interesting, not you!

Hyperactivity: Your body might need to move MORE than other kids. Sitting still might feel really, really hard. Your body has extra energy!

Impulsivity: You might do or say things before thinking about them. Your brain moves fast! Sometimes too fast to think first.

Working Memory: You might forget things easily, even things from five minutes ago. Your brain doesn't hold onto information as well as other brains.

Emotions: Your feelings might be BIGGER and STRONGER than other kids' feelings. When you're happy, you're really happy! When you're sad or angry, those feelings can feel huge.

Time: Time might feel weird to you. An hour might feel like five minutes, or five minutes might feel like an hour. Your brain doesn't feel time the same way other brains do.

Starting Tasks: Beginning something might feel really hard, even when you want to do it. Your brain gets stuck and doesn't know how to start.

Not everyone with ADHD has all of these! ADHD is different for every person.

Is ADHD bad?

No! ADHD isn't bad. It makes some things harder, but it makes other things easier.

Things ADHD might make harder:

- Sitting still in class
- Remembering homework
- Focusing on boring stuff
- Waiting your turn
- Controlling big feelings
- Keeping track of time

Things ADHD might make easier:

- Being creative and coming up with cool ideas
- Noticing details other people miss
- Thinking fast when things change
- Being passionate about your interests
- Having lots of energy and enthusiasm
- Trying new things without being scared

The same brain that makes homework hard might make art easy. The same brain that makes sitting still hard might be great at sports or building or creating.

Can ADHD be fixed?

ADHD isn't something to "fix" because you're not broken! But you CAN learn strategies that help. You can learn to work WITH your ADHD brain instead of against it.

Things that help:

- Tools and systems (like special spots for your stuff, timers, checklists)
- Strategies (like breaking big tasks into tiny steps, using fidgets, taking movement breaks)
- Accommodations at school (like extra time, quiet spaces, wiggle seats)
- Sometimes medication (some kids take medicine that helps their ADHD brain focus better)
- Understanding (when you and the people around you understand how your brain works, everything gets easier!)

Will I have ADHD forever?

Yes! ADHD is part of how your brain works. It doesn't go away when you grow up.

But here's the good news: as you get older, you get better at managing it. You learn what strategies work for you. You find activities and jobs that work well with your ADHD brain. You build a life that fits how YOU work!

Many successful adults have ADHD. Artists, entrepreneurs, athletes, scientists, teachers, doctors, and all kinds of other people. They learned to work with their ADHD brains, and you can too!

The most important thing to remember:

You are not broken. You are not bad. You are not lazy. You are not stupid.

You have an ADHD brain, and that brain works differently.

Sometimes that makes things harder. Sometimes that makes things easier.

You're learning strategies to help with the hard stuff. And you're discovering what your ADHD brain is really good at!

You're not broken. You're different.

And different is okay.

TIPS FOR PARENTS

Your child has ADHD. You're doing your best to support them, but it's hard. These tips can help.

Understand What ADHD Really Is

ADHD is neurological, not behavioral. Your child isn't choosing to forget, interrupt, or lose things. Their brain literally works differently. When you understand this, everything changes.

What ADHD affects:

- Executive functions (planning, organizing, starting tasks, working memory)
- Impulse control (thinking before acting or speaking)
- Emotional regulation (managing big feelings)

- Attention regulation (focusing on boring tasks, not hyperfocusing on interesting ones)
- Sensory needs (movement, stimulation)
- Time perception

This means: "Try harder" doesn't work. Punishment doesn't work. Shame definitely doesn't work. Your child IS trying. They need different strategies, not more effort.

Create External Structures

ADHD brains struggle with internal organization. So create EXTERNAL systems that organize for them.

Examples:

- Visual schedules and checklists (pictures help!)
- Designated spots for everything (ALWAYS the same spot)
- Timers to make time visible
- Alarms and reminders
- Written instructions, not just verbal
- Organizational tools (bins, labels, color coding)

The goal: Don't expect your child's brain to remember and organize. Build systems that remember and organize for them.

Break Everything Into Tiny Steps

Big tasks overwhelm ADHD brains. Break everything into steps so small they feel easy.

Instead of "clean your room," try:

1. Pick up one toy
2. Put one piece of clothing in hamper
3. Make your bed
4. Put one book on shelf

Instead of "do your homework," try:

- Do problem #1
- Do problem #2
- Continue one at a time

The first step should be SO easy they can't say no. Once they've started, continuing is easier.

Use Positive Reinforcement

ADHD kids hear "no," "stop," and "don't" all day long. They're drowning in criticism. Actively look for things to praise.

Catch them doing things right:

- "You remembered to put your backpack in its spot!"
- "You waited your turn before talking!"
- "You worked for ten whole minutes without getting distracted!"

Even small things deserve recognition. ADHD kids are trying SO hard. Notice their effort, not just results.

Movement Is Not Misbehavior

Your child's body NEEDS to move. Fighting this makes everything harder.

Instead of forcing stillness:

- Provide movement breaks every 15-20 minutes
- Use fidget tools (stress balls, putty, smooth stones)
- Let them stand or kneel while working
- Use wiggle seats or yoga balls
- Build movement into routines (jumping jacks before homework, running between tasks)

Movement helps ADHD brains focus. It's not distraction, it's medicine.

Homework Doesn't Have To Be A Battle

Homework is extra hard for ADHD kids. Make it easier:

- Remove all distractions first (TV off, phone away, quiet space)
- Break homework into 10-15 minute chunks with breaks
- Start with the hardest subject when energy is highest
- Use timers to make time visible
- Allow movement breaks
- Consider doing some homework at school if possible
- Talk to the teacher about reducing homework load if it's taking unreasonable amounts of time

If homework is taking twice as long as it should, that's a sign your child needs accommodations, not more pressure.

Emotional Dysregulation Is Real

ADHD kids feel emotions more intensely than neurotypical kids. Small problems feel like disasters. They're not being dramatic.

Help them manage big feelings:

- Teach them to notice early warning signs (tight chest, hot face, clenched fists)
- Create a feelings scale (1-10) so they can identify intensity
- Have calming tools ready (deep breaths, cold water, tight hugs, quiet space)
- Intervene at 5, not 10 (catch feelings before explosion)
- Never punish emotional dysregulation (it's neurological, not defiance)

Model calm responses. Your calm helps them calm.

Get School Accommodations

Your child is entitled to accommodations under Section 504 or an IEP. Don't wait. Get them formalized.

Common helpful accommodations:

- Extended time on tests

- Preferential seating (front of class, away from distractions)
- Movement breaks
- Fidget tools
- Breaks between subjects
- Reduced homework load
- Written instructions in addition to verbal
- Extra time to copy notes
- Use of calculator, spellcheck, or other tools

Document your child's challenges and request a formal evaluation. Accommodations aren't special treatment, they're equity.

Accept That Your Child Is Different

Stop comparing your child to neurotypical kids. Your ADHD child will not develop the same way or at the same pace.

They might:

- Still need help with organization in middle school when peers don't
- Struggle with independence longer
- Need more reminders and support
- Be emotionally younger than their age
- Excel in some areas and struggle in others

That's okay. Different timelines don't mean failure. They mean different.

Find What They're Good At

ADHD makes some things hard. But ADHD brains are often excellent at other things.

Look for:

- Creativity (art, music, building, storytelling)
- Hyperfocus on interests (when they love something, they REALLY love it)
- Quick thinking in emergencies
- Noticing details others miss
- Enthusiasm and passion
- Trying new things fearlessly

Nurture their strengths. Let them spend time doing what they're good at. Success in one area builds confidence for tackling hard areas.

Take Care of Yourself

Parenting an ADHD child is exhausting. You cannot pour from an empty cup.

You need:

- Breaks
- Support (therapist, support group, understanding friends)
- Compassion for yourself (you're doing your best)
- To let go of perfection
- Help (you don't have to do this alone)

Your child needs you healthy and calm more than they need you perfect.

Remember The Big Picture

Right now, homework and chores and behavior feel overwhelming. But your child will grow up. They will learn to manage their ADHD. They will find careers and lives that work for their brains.

Your job right now:

- Help them understand their brain
- Teach them strategies
- Build their confidence
- Advocate for accommodations
- Love them as they are

ADHD kids grow into ADHD adults who thrive. Not despite their ADHD, but by learning to work with it.

Your child isn't broken. They're different. And with understanding, strategies, and support, different can absolutely thrive.

RESOURCES

Resources for Kids

Books:

- *The Survival Guide for Kids with ADHD* by John F. Taylor

- *Learning to Slow Down & Pay Attention* by Kathleen G. Nadeau and Ellen B. Dixon
- *Putting on the Brakes* by Patricia O. Quinn and Judith M. Stern

Websites:

- Understood.org (information about ADHD and learning differences)
- ADDitude Magazine (additudemag.com - articles for kids with ADHD)

RESOURCES FOR PARENTS

Books by Richard Bass:

ADHD Kids: 12 Success Stories

Stories of Kids with ADHD Who Found What Works Including Easy Activities and Strategies for Ages 7-11

Available on Amazon

The ADHD Parenting Guide for Boys: From Toddlers to Teens

Discover How to Respond Appropriately to Different Behavioral Situations

Available on Amazon

The ADHD Parenting Guide for Girls: From Toddlers to Teens

Discover How to Respond Appropriately to Different Behavioral Situations

Available on Amazon

A Beginner's Guide on Parenting Children with ADHD

A Modern Approach to Understand and Lead your Hyperactive Child to Success

Available on Amazon

For a complete list of Richard's books on ADHD, autism, and neurodivergent support, visit amazon.com/author/richardbass

Understanding ADHD:

CHADD (Children and Adults with ADHD)

Website: chadd.org

The leading national organization for ADHD education, advocacy, and support

ADDitude Magazine

Website: additudemag.com

Articles, webinars, and resources for parents of children with ADHD

Understood.org

Website: understood.org

Information on ADHD and learning differences for parents

Russell Barkley's YouTube Channel

Dr. Barkley is a leading ADHD researcher with excellent parent lectures

Thriving with Richard Bass (YouTube Channel)

Created by the author of this book, videos on ADHD, gentle parenting, and neurodivergent topics

School Support:

Wrightslaw

Website: wrightslaw.com

Information on special education law, IEPs, and 504 plans

Understood.org IEP/504 Resources

Website: understood.org

Guides for navigating school accommodations

Finding Professional Support:
To find an ADHD specialist:

- Ask your pediatrician for referrals
- Check Psychology Today's therapist finder (filter by ADHD)
- Contact local CHADD chapters for provider recommendations
- Check your insurance provider directory

Types of professionals who can help:

- Pediatricians (diagnosis, medication management)
- Child psychiatrists (diagnosis, medication management)
- Child psychologists (diagnosis, therapy, testing)
- Licensed therapists/counselors (therapy, coping strategies)
- Educational therapists (homework help, study skills)
- ADHD coaches (organization, life skills)

Parent Support:

CHADD Parent Support Groups

Find local or virtual groups at chadd.org

Facebook Groups:

- ADHD Parents Together
- Parents of Children with ADHD

Remember: You don't have to do this alone. Connecting with other parents who understand helps immensely.

Crisis Support:

988 Suicide and Crisis Lifeline

Call or text 988

24/7 support for mental health crises

Crisis Text Line

Text HOME to 741741

24/7 text-based crisis support

National Alliance on Mental Illness (NAMI)

Website: nami.org

Call: 1-800-950-NAMI (6264)

Education, support, and crisis resources

ABOUT THE AUTHOR

Richard Bass is a special education teacher, bestselling author, and advocate for neurodivergent children and families. With over a decade of classroom experience and more than 20 published books focused on ADHD, autism, sensory processing, and gentle parenting, Richard has helped hundreds of thousands of families worldwide better understand and support neurodivergent children.

Through his Richard Bass author brand and RBG Publishing, Richard creates practical, compassionate resources grounded in both research and real-world experience. His books have sold over 100,000 copies and are used by parents, educators, and mental health professionals across the globe.

Richard specializes in translating complex neurodevelopmental concepts into accessible, actionable strategies. His work emphasizes understanding neurodivergent children as different rather than deficient, building systems that work for how their brains actually function, and celebrating neurodiversity rather than trying to "fix" it.

When not writing or teaching, Richard can be found experimenting with new parenting approaches with his own child, creating content for his YouTube channel "Thriving with Richard Bass," or researching the latest developments in ADHD, autism, and child development.

Richard holds degrees in education and special education, with additional training in Cognitive Behavioral Therapy (CBT), Dialectical Behavior Therapy (DBT), and social-emotional learning approaches.

Connect with Richard:

- YouTube: Thriving with Richard Bass
- Instagram/TikTok/Facebook: @richardbassauthor
- Amazon: amazon.com/author/richardbass

Join Richard's email list for bonus content and newsletters at richardbassauthor.com

THE END

Thank you for reading ADHD Kids: 12 Success Stories!